Through everything we endured,
I learned this one lesson.
Home, after all, isn't a place.
It's a heartbeat.

(we're) HOME less

Making Home Wherever We Go

Brooke Sailer .

ISBN-13: 978-1726416344 (CreateSpace-Assigned)
ISBN-10: 1726416348
BISAC: Self-Help / Motivational & Inspirational

CONTENTS

....

BONUS CONTENT

WHAT WOMEN ARE SAYING

....

When I read this, I wanted to weep. The last line made my heart
feel so full. Well done, Brooke. Your storytelling is reassuring,
powerful, and emotional. This is a priceless treasure. Thank
you for your vulnerability. It has been so empowering.

CHERI

As I finished reading Brooke's book, tears streaming down my
cheeks, I exclaimed, "Yes! This is so good!" She has a way of
making you feel like you can conquer the world, even when life is
far from perfect. As someone who feels like my life is transitioning,
I'm reminded that my home is not my house…it's my heart. It's
my family. And it makes me want to be home for others.

DANA

It's our human nature—we all want to know that someone
else went through it. Reading this book gave me that
I'm not alone feeling. I'm so glad I read this.

LAUREN

I read this and said, "Whoa. So good. Preach!" I love Brooke's heart.

CAMEY

We live in a day and time when women compare themselves to
others more than ever before. This leads to unnecessary expectation
and pressure to have it all together, when rarely any of us do.
Thank you, Brooke, for this book. It is truly 1000% relatable.

TRACEY

Brooke! When I finished reading your manuscript, I felt very
emotional. I didn't think I would. We are on the brink of transition,
but have no idea what our next steps will be. No plans, no "next
thing," no list for me to check off. We're just trying to be faithful
where we are right now and in the waiting. This is why your book
hit me so hard in the best way. There's a sacredness in choosing
to live a life of faith in the midst of whatever comes and in
relinquishing control over what I used to think I wanted my life to
be. Don't you love how your priorities change with some of these
in-between times? I'm so thankful for you. You will reach so many
hearts with your honesty and reassurance, just as you did mine.

SHANNON

"Brooke brings hope as a speaker, author and friend. Hope
that life CAN change, WILL change and hope that
it will all be for my greatest personal growth."

KATIE

Wow, I wish I'd had this book a year-and-a-half ago! I prepared
my house to look its best for my friends to come over and listen
to Brooke talk about the concepts in her first book, This Thing
Called Home. Two days later, my downstairs flooded and we were
displaced for an unknown amount of time. Weeks and weeks passed.
With three children under our roof, it was a very difficult time. It
definitely challenged my ideas about home. I had to reevaluate what
home meant and how to bring peace no matter where we were located.
Many times I felt like I failed. The truth Brooke shares in (We're)
Home.less is spot on, and if we ever go through something like
that again, I will have the confidence and peace that I lacked before.

JOANNA

Join Brooke Sailer as she takes you on her journey from a successful minimalism mom to a living-in-the-moment one. Home.less is a deep dive into more than un-cluttering your closets, it will unclutter your heart creating a place, a space, and a new definition of home. You are going to love it! I highly recommend it for every mom.

MONA CORWIN, SPEAKER, AUTHOR,
MOM-MENTOR, BALANCEDMOMLIFE.COM

ONE NAVIGATOR'S STORY

....

I first read Brooke's book several months before a major unforeseen transition in my life. And during that season of my very own home-lessness, my mind returned to this book and its inspirations.

You see, my family was renovating a new house, and it was horribly behind schedule. No matter what we did to try to keep this project on track, it fell behind. Our house sold quicker than we expected, so we got stuck, just like Brooke. For us, this season lasted over two months.

The day we packed the bedrooms, the kids' toys, and everything else, we sent it to a storage unit. I fought back tears that day, remembering all the memories made in each room as I walked through the house one last time.

The only plan that we could secure on such short notice was to move into my sister's attic. My husband and I and our two kids would be in the one room upstairs. My sister, her husband, and three kids would be downstairs. This was supposed to be a short interlude between our old home and new home, but our contractor continually fell behind schedule. Two weeks quickly became two months, and I finally hit my breaking point. Again, I thought of Brooke's book. Unplanned scenarios happen to many moms like me all the time.

At my lowest point, I was emotionally spent. I told my husband that I was taking the kids to my parents' house in Florida. I needed a place to make a home for my kids. I packed our belongings into our one suitcase and headed to the airport. We stayed there for two weeks. The kids fell into their routine for the first time since we sold our home. It was such a temporary time of comfort.

As the project continued to encounter delays, the kids missed their daddy, so it was back to Texas we went. Florida was hot, but when we got back to Texas, it was *unbelievably* hot. The day we returned was the hottest day in Texas had seen in six years: 115 degrees.

When we finally arrived at my sister's house, it was well past my kid's bedtime. They were melting down. We headed up the stairs. I was eager to put them to bed and remake this attic into home for a few more days. But as I opened the door, I discovered the air conditioning failed. I checked the thermostat. It was at 96 degrees. Cue another emotional breakdown for me.

My kids watched me cry hysterically. It was all too much. I had held it together for too long. So in that moment, I made a plan. I remembered that Brooke and her family were on vacation. I asked to stay in their guest room, which Brooke had offered to us once before. Within minutes, we made the plan to leave my sister's house and set up home at The Sailer home.

My most important job was to take care of my two kids. Yes, I was sad. But it was time to spring into action and move forward. Early on in our displacement, I sense the changes and lack of routine wearing on my children. My first priority, no matter where we were staying, was to provide an environment that felt comfortable and safe.

After the kids were in bed, I cried again. I mourned the house we sold, the never-ending house renovation, and the discomfort of not having a home. But also, for the first time, I was finally able breathe. In this house—although not ours—we were all comfortable. I knew I could get back to a routine with the kids and have some fun.

By the time Brooke and her family returned from vacation, our re-modeling project was completed and we were busy moving in. Just like that, the season that seemed to last forever was over.

We make plans. We do our best to stick to those plans. And with toddlers in tow, sticking to the plan helps alleviate chaos. However, when you're in transition, plans change on the fly. You learn how to adapt immediately. You learn how to bounce back from failed plans. Brooke had to do that, too.

Yep!

This book will push you to see home where you are. It will encourage you to see the blessing in every aspect of your scenario. This book will teach you that home can be anywhere, just as it taught me. Everything we endured made me appreciate our new home even more.

The plans now? Fill this new home with memories and hold on to the lessons I learned.

Brooke's latest book is a must-read for anyone that is in a season of transition. In our own season of homelessness, remembering her book brought me so much comfort. A temporary place to stay helped a lot, too.

Proud to know you.   —TIFFANY

xoxo,
B

CHANGE CAN BE GOOD
INTRODUCTION

....

If you've ever felt alone, displaced, overwhelmed, disappointed, or uncomfortable—and if you have no idea how to be a mom during a season like that—this book is for you.

I loaded the kids into the minivan and buckled them as quickly as I could. I didn't want to get caught in the rain. It was an unusually cloudy day in early January, and I sensed a storm coming. North Texas is mostly sunny with a side of watch-out-there's-a-crazy-hail-storm-or-tornado-on-its-way. I walked around to the driver's seat and jumped in. But before I pulled out of the parking lot, I checked the weather. No hail. It seemed it would just be cloudy all day. I determined that I was being too analytical and decided to stick with my original plan. We were going to the grocery store.

I grabbed a small, hand-held cart.

"But, what about the big cart, mama?"

My middle daughter, Bella, looked up at me with hopeful eyes. "Not this time, babe. The hotel has a small fridge, so we'll just pick up a few things. Besides, I don't know how long we'll be there."

I hid my uncertainty from the kids as much as I could, but I couldn't hide the truth from myself. I didn't know how long we'd be in the hotel. That thought terrified me. I filled my small grocery cart as the kids roamed through the aisles alongside me.

My intention was to grab fruit (everyone loves fruit), some lunch meat for sandwiches (another go-to with little clean up), and a few snacks. Our favorites are popcorn, pretzels, and trail mix. I landed on carrots and hummus, too, because, you know, veggies are important.

As we checked out, the cashier made small talk with my kids.

"I've never seen you here before. Do you live around here?"

"We're homeless." My oldest daughter didn't skip a beat with her reply.

I smiled and nodded. But I died inside.

We returned to the hotel, where we had been living for just two days, carried our five grocery bags across the lobby to the elevator, rode up to the 4th floor, and walked down the hall to our room. I settled the kids with a bowl of popcorn, a coloring book, and crayons.

I locked myself in the bathroom and sobbed.

My daughter was right. We were, essentially, homeless.

The problem wasn't financial, it was circumstantial. We found ourselves in the midst of a major life change. We had some life-changing decisions to make. This season of transition was wildly uncomfortable for my nature, which is typically, *ahem*, put together. Coupled with a slew of undetermined details and potential opportunities that didn't manifest quickly enough, this transition deemed us residents of a local hotel. With our belongings in a storage unit, we waited for life to return to normal.

Months before, we intentionally deviated from our suburban life and took an extended vacation that we affectionately called "the sabbatical." We set aside the necessary funds to live completely without the pressures of career. We planned to homeschool to alleviate the pressure of routine.

Our life encountered a natural invitation to adventure when my husband sold his company and we simultaneously wanted to take advantage of the profitable real estate market and sell our home. Rather than move across town, we opted to use this in-between time for an extended trip.

As our sabbatical came to a close, we scoured real estate websites for a new home. My husband perused new job opportunities, none of which had solidified. We grew increasingly uncomfortable in our decision as to where we should purchase another home and which job opportunity would be the next best thing. Stepping out of the sabbatical and returning to a more established home life was the place we got stuck. So we decided to press pause so we could breathe and clear our heads. And that translated into hotel living for a few weeks.

The waiting of this season didn't feel painful, it felt lonely and confusing. And also odd. What made it difficult for me was the way I had deceived myself into believing I was an "expert" homemaker.

Over the course of my married life, I mastered my cooking, cleaning, organizing, and decorating skills. I loved my hard-earned rhythms, routines, and skill set. They became part of my identity as a mother. I especially loved hospitality. Fancy dinner parties were a major part of our life before the sabbatical. Now, as my tears fell onto the floor of the hotel bathroom, I craved the familiarity of my house. It was a house I learned and fought to love beyond many insecurities.

Can change *really* be good? Because, in this moment, all I felt was sadness.

The sadness was perpetuated by the uncertainty of what was to come. Maybe if I knew this "stuck" place would only last a week or so, I would have easily endured. I might have even found joy in it. The sabbatical was exciting; but coming out of it and trying to re-establish a normal life beyond vacation was proving to be more difficult than I expected.

I counted on my motherhood "working" because of the routines I cultivated. Formulating a bulletproof process for every tiny thing necessary to care for my children's needs was the way I functioned before. As I saw my ideas for routine crumble, I had to adapt. Honestly, I had to grieve. Perhaps my identity as a mother was synonymous with being a good homemaker. Being homeless meant that I had no place to carry out these routines and skills I thought I needed.

I truly found myself wondering how my motherhood would survive such drastic transition after (rocky) transition. Everything I thought I knew about motherhood shifted: the routines, what children need, and what a family needs. It was immensely unsettling.

The good news is that I survived. It was wildly different than I imagined, but I got through it.

What I came to learn was that, beyond survival, I was able to look at the basic needs of my children with clarity and fulfill them, no matter where we were located physically. The foundation I set in nurturing them in our home translated beautifully to making home wherever we went.

Here's what to expect from our story.

I lived through plenty of failed plans, a terrible move, slip-ups, and set-backs. But it was not without solutions and strategies, which I will share with you. Even deeper, I hope to relay our family's real experience of leaving the norm and the freedom that comes with letting go of the least important stuff in order to cling more tightly to what matters most.

When you've read the book in its entirety, I hope you will see this clearly. More than anything, during this time I was forced to redefine home in light of shifting parts. I finally landed on what home means to me. If you've found yourself in the midst of any major life transition, I hope it helps you make home anyway. Home, after all, isn't a place. It's a heartbeat.

But before you dive in, I'd like to offer a warning. If you read my first book, *This Thing Called Home*, you might read *(We're) Home.less* and wonder if I'm actually the same person. I'm happy to report...I'm not. I suppose that's the wonderful thing about growth. I'm not the same person today that I was even just yesterday. Please don't hold it against me. Sure, there are times I put a little order or routine back into our life if it makes us all happier. But the order and routine I establish for my family don't define me anymore.

I've walked some harder roads. My intentions have been tested. I'm proud to say that I love the concept of home now more than ever. I don't have it all figured out, and maybe you don't either. I hope, more than anything, that my story will help you know you're not alone. And this girl is happy to give you a peek into my hardest season as a mom.

Just moved?
Lost a job?
Anticipating a move?
Waiting on transition?
Living somewhere temporarily, waiting on a permanent location?
Not sure how to navigate change?
Resistant to life's changes?
Trying to be an exceptional mom without a home?

Yes, this book is for you. *It's gonna be ok.*

I don't love the fact that things have to change. But friends, change is an inevitable part of life. I'm still trying to make peace with that. Maybe adapting to change—or just plain standing tall when everything around you is crumbling—is a bigger part of motherhood than I ever thought.

If you read my first book, you'll find that marrying the concepts I taught then with the ideas I share here will give you a much deeper understanding of home.

Remember that time you changed the narrative, embraced possibilities, and re-made home? This book begs the questions:

What happens when the narrative shifts?

When impossibilities loom?

When home has to be redefined completely?

I think something beautiful and miraculous happens.

I think something powerful and sacred happens.

I think something brave and lovely can happen, eventually, on the other side of uncertainty. It's just a bit past adaptability and through some mucky waters of disappointment and heartache, too.

Most importantly, the foundation of courage you set when you read *This Thing Called Home* will launch you into a countless new opportunities to try it out because life is full of moving parts. And if you haven't read that book yet, it will be the best backstory as to why home matters to me and why, when it disappeared, my world fell apart.

I've heard it said that walking into a season of uncertainty feels like jumping off a cliff in the dark. I know I felt that way several times. I kept thinking it would break me entirely. But actually, it was time to spread my wings and fly.

So when you feel like everything's falling apart, just remember that you're only falling into something new. You're going to soar, figure it out, and make it to the other side because…change can be good.

Let's jump.

Brooke

FAILED PLANS

PART ONE

....

"Quit letting who you were talk you out of who you're becoming."
BOB GOFF[1]

who you're is becoming beautiful.

THE WORST-MOVE-EVER
CHAPTER ONE

....

Since writing a book on home, traveling, and speaking to countless women on the topic of homemaking, I realized something terrible. I accidentally became a self-proclaimed expert on all things *home*.

Don't know how to properly fold a fitted sheet? I'm your girl.

Not sure how to corral an out-of-control pantry? Gotcha covered.

Overwhelmed by too many toys and constant messes? Problem solved.

Feeling discouraged by an always-too-much job as a stay-at-home mom and can't figure out what to tell yourself? I'm here with journaling, lists, and charts for that, too. *check!*

If there's anything I fought to become, it was an *exceptional* stay-at-home mom.

❧ HOW I GOT HERE

My husband, Scott, and I married fourteen years ago. He scooped me up when I was in college. We laugh about it now, but the first thing he said on our first date was, "Brooke, don't freak out. I'm looking for a wife." *Ha!*

I died. Well, I didn't *really* die. But you know.

He took me back to my dorm building after dinner. I floated down a flight of steps and darted directly into my friends' room.

"He said, 'Don't freak out, but I'm looking for a wife.' He said that! He *actually* said that!"

I was shouting. I was shout-speaking. You know when you talk so loudly and so fast that the sentence has no punctuation? Yeah, that.

My girlfriends slipped notes under my door and in my mailbox for the next week that read, "Don't freak out!"

We laughed so hard about it. I didn't keep my cool. I was completely uncool about this entire thing.

And over time, it became more evident. He was beyond ready for a settled life. But I was not. He cooked gourmet food (still does), had a dedicated fitness routine and a six pack to prove it, a good job, a salary, and was in the process of buying a home. I was really good at making macaroni and cheese. Sometimes.

I was his dream girl: creative, driven, 4.0 student, creative, a brunette with curly hair (his type, he claims), and did I mention creative?

He said, "You seem really artsy and I like that."

I wore a teal trench coat to coffee on our first date. He thought I was really artsy, since he assumed a Boston college girl would show up in a preppy polo-shirt dress.

We had a whirlwind romance that lead to a marriage, a home, and a whole life. But in the beginning, my homemaking skills were nil. I neglected the laundry for so long that it molded in the washing machine. I thought that was normal. "Artsy" was awesome until we had two kids and I still was making macaroni and cheese on the regular, letting the laundry pile up, and dusting maybe once a year. I *really* didn't know any different.

Somewhere around our fifth year of marriage, I felt really incapable. I thought my life was a complete bust. I was a failure. I hated my under-skilled homemaking and motherhood. I thought everyone else was just "talented," until I realized I could do it…if I was willing to learn.

And I did. During the following five years I taught myself to cook, clean regularly, and organize everything in sight. The biggest lesson I learned was to replace the false belief that others were talented in this arena and that I was not with the truth that if anyone could do it, I could do it, too. So I did.

I pushed hard for routines that worked. I created systems around my house for taking care of my family. I thrived on structure. I was proud of how I constructed my own skill set from scratch.

❧ FROM EXPERT TO HUMAN

After years of feeling like a failure, I finally felt like an expert. I saw other women in the same overwhelmed-and-uninspired boat and became eager to teach them what I learned. I called myself a "SAHM coach." All my knowledge was wonderful, until I moved and all the systems and routines became impossible and unimportant. Oops, I forgot about that little thing in life called…*change*.

I gave my whole heart to helping others thrive at home, but maybe that comes with the false perception that I have it all together. Perhaps it left the impression that I shouldn't be invited for dinner if your pantry is disorganized and there's laundry on the dining room table. But it happens to me, too. *Truth.*

We still want to judge moms with clean houses, happy faces, and tidy children. We do. Especially on a bad day, we want to dehumanize people and blame them for the "fake" standards they set that keep us from measuring up.

When this negativity, blame shifting, and poor self-talk sets in, there's usually one remedy. Humanity. Keep people human. This is part of the reason I'm writing this book. I'm keeping myself human.

I faced my own humanity, weaknesses, struggles, and insecurities that surfaced during our season of transition. And now that I've filled you in on my journey up to this point, where do we go from here?

Here's where I think we begin.

Compassion.
Listening.
Better questions.
More seeing.
More pausing.
Less blaming.
Less comparing.
More kindness.
More life together.
Less expectation.
Less limitation.
Less self-judgement.
Less worries and fears.
Less...home.

less is more.

I had some successes, some failures, and a lot of learning. But mostly, I had seeing. I lived for the moment, looked for courage, and fought for lessons to be understood and applied. It was both horribly unstable and incredibly thrilling. It was exciting and life-giving and down right exhausting. Often, the moments and big feelings collided all at once.

Have you had moments when you were in the middle of the juxtaposition of hard things and amazing things? I find that we tend to want security, joy, and contentment, but don't always realize that they often come alongside pain, change, uncertainty, or sadness. At least, that's how it happened for me.

❧ HANDLING CHANGE

How do you handle change? If you're anything like me, change throws everything into a tailspin.

You just got the baby to sleep through the night, then a new neighbor moves in next door. This neighbor loves practicing drums in the garage right by the baby's window. *Change.*

It's mid-September and the kids are settled into a new school. You're on a roll: packing lunches, carpooling, and supervising play dates with the same sweet friends. Then, out of nowhere, your husband's boss says he needs to move him to a different territory. *Change.*

Your oldest turns 19 this year. All along his plan has been to live at home for two more years and attend a community college. But then, he learns of a scholarship potential, applies on a whim, is accepted, and decides to move eight states away. He leaves in six weeks. *Change.*

Oh, change. Life is full of change. I know I won't be able to cover it all. But if there's one thing this book does, I hope it will help you embrace change with grace.

❧ LIFE'S ABOUT TO CHANGE

The series of big life events weren't neatly spaced out the way I would have preferred. They say that when it rains, it pours. That's exactly what happened during the month of June 2016.

I wrote a book, my husband sold his company, we put our house on the market, we packed up our life, and we moved to Washington state to begin a sabbatical. It was one full month.

I wrote a book. I signed up for a self-publishing course on the first of May. I knew it would be extremely sacrificial for me to keep up with the ongoing homework and coursework with four small children at home. But something in my spirit said I needed to do this. I believe it was a fruit of my media fast. You see, in April of that year—inspired by a book I just read—I determined to take a 30-day media fast. During those 30 days, I purposed to steer clear of all social media and many interactions or commitments. I slowed my life down to a halt and discovered pockets of precious time I was previously wasting. A remarkable amount of clarity followed. I had a few dreams I wanted to give myself permission to pursue.

Writing a book was at the top of that bucket list. When a friend suggested Self-Publishing School[2], I jumped on it. I knew we would put the house up for sale during the summer in an attempt to attract young families and potential buyers who typically move in the summertime. I just didn't realize it would happen so fast.

Within a few minutes of listing our house, we had a full-price offer. Within the first hour of it being on the market, 13 showings were scheduled for that very day. Within yet another hour, an additional five showings were booked. Offers above asking price came in quickly, and by the end of our home's very first day on the market, we had a wide variety of best offers to choose from. I was shocked.

We started the packing process right away. Keeping up with normal life, homeschooling, and my self-publishing coursework would prove to be too much for me.

The well-kept house, hard-earned routines, and efficiencies you read about in This Thing Called Home were unknowingly just a temporary thing.

My husband of fourteen years is a serial entrepreneur with endless ideas for projects and work. When we married, he forewarned me that there would be no place he could settle forever. I was probably too distracted keeping our life afloat to realize that our uprooting was just around the corner. Suddenly, with great urgency we felt the push toward the sabbatical we were saving for, to postpone buying a new home until after the sabbatical, and to give him time and space to pause and consider his next career move.

Looking back, I knew it was just a matter of time before there was a next big idea. After all, we had lived a suburban life for five years. Our kids, at ages 9, 7, 5, and 2, were officially out of the needy baby stage.

I didn't process the unavoidable difficulty at the time we started talking about a transition out of our dream home. I sort of understood the monumental nature of it and acknowledged how Scott had sacrificed his wanderlust in order to give me a sense of security when our babies were small.

Having immersed myself in the re-creation of frameworks for possibilities at home, my new self was embracing these changes with gusto. I was positive, courageous, and open to learning. I was *in it to win it*, you could say.

I had plans. Big ones. Good ones. I had ideas. I was committed. I was working it. I was putting my whole self into a great move. I was controlling it. And, certainly, it would go just as planned.

It didn't. It most certainly didn't. Not even a little bit.

Three weeks before our big move, I taught the most in-depth home-making class I had ever taught. Teaching one-hour sessions on home organization was a regular part of my life, but I wanted to branch out and cover a wider variety of topics centered around home. I invited 12 ladies to spend a few hours with me in my home. I prepared teaching workbooks that I had bound at the local print shop across the street. I covered growth mindset, home organization, hospitality, becoming a doer, and so much more.

I even introduced them to a new recipe and cooked dinner in front of them as we set the table together and enjoyed a kid-free dinner. And this was the beginning of my heart being pulled to do more than just my own homemaking and mothering.

For a long time, I bought the lie that if you're a mom, you can't do anything but be a mom. For so many of us, however, motherhood is equally too much and not enough. Deep down, if we're honest, many of us would admit that we feel unfilled in the redundancy of life as a stay-at-home mom. Between continual chores, child-rearing, and the pressure to do it all well, we are left with wanting to do something for ourselves. Am I right?

It was during the early stages of writing my first book and taking on a heftier teaching schedule that our life began to shift. Yes, the circumstances were about to change, but I was also changing. I finally gave myself permission to say "yes!" to productivity beyond the work within the walls of my home.

This new-found freedom I experienced as I helped stay-at-home moms catapulted me into even more opportunities to say yes.

Yes, I'll teach this class. Yes, I'll teach another class. Yes, I'll make a workbook to go with it and cook dinner for everyone. And I'll stay on top of my own housework, wean my baby, homeschool our two oldest children, and begin preparations for a move.

It was a season of *yes* after many years of *no*.

And in that freedom, when I was ready to be brave, to write and market a book, to make my dreams a priority, and to succumb to my husband's desire for this sabbatical, I overdid it. I had no sense of balance. Emotionally, I was far-removed from the work our move would demand. I didn't know what I didn't know.

❧ THE MOVE

At the genesis of the moving process, I was Brooke-level organized. I labeled well. I made a chart. It had something to do with colored duct tape and coinciding rooms. I found this inspiration on Pinterest, of course, and I was committed. But as each box became more and more like a jigsaw puzzle, and as the truck morphed into an epic game of real-life Tetris, I lost it. Nothing fit. My colored system failed because things fit in boxes strangely.

The girls' baby doll cradle needed a large rectangular box, but the only thing that fit in it were a few blankets and a living room lamp. It wasn't 100% full, so I added in a sleeping bag from the garage and a few dishes. *Oops. What color duct tape does this box need?*

Have you ever moved before? Have you had the experience of things fitting awkwardly in boxes or not in any boxes at all so you roll it in bubble wrap and hope for the best?

My labeling skills dwindled from masterful to elementary. The last 50 boxes were labeled things like: *master bedroom junk drawer, miscellaneous, to be organized, random stuff,* and I'm losing my mind. The movers → giggled and joked with me about the crazy labeling, especially the one that read: *I'm losing my mind.*

for real

Lastly, I resorted to the most vulnerable details: *mostly towels, but also vases and a sheet, a picture frame, and the leftovers from the downstairs closet.*

Ugh. My home organization expertise failed me. My insides were boiling. Yet I also found relief in laughing at myself. What else does one do in such a moment?

Can you relate?

Have you ever moved?

Or does life feel like a mess of moving boxes, some tightly organized and labeled, and others haphazardly thrown together for survival's sake? Life comes at us from many angles. It's full of change, whether or not our physical location changes. Not everything in this one category fits neatly in a box.

Our lives are neither predictable nor perfectly fitting.

If you have physically packed up and made a move, is it always this crazy? For us, it was pure craziness. Pure chaos. Admittedly, maybe life with four kids is just crazy, and anything plus four kids is too much at times.

Should I have done this a certain way? What do other people do? What on Earth is that and how do I pack it? Was I supposed to consult my Pinterest board for this move?

As a fan of all things successful and efficient, I will not declare this move a failure, but a learning experience. Right? *Are you sighing in relief that I'm normal?* Oh good, me too.

❧ SO NAÏVE

Since I'm not a controller by nature, fairly easy-going, and intro-verted, my internal struggles (thankfully) weren't being taken out on others. They were just eating away at my insides. I was eating chocolate and procrastinating just like the rest of you.

On five separate occasions during the course of 24 hours, Scott went back to the local hardware store for more tape.

Was one of my kids eating it? Why is the tape disappearing? How much more tape do I need? How much should I have bought the first time? Do I need stock in this company? Can you buy it in bulk for a discount? Did we really run out of tape again? I told you to buy the big package!

I hadn't moved with four kids before, and honestly, I was part naïve and part "letting it go" because of my book deadlines.

What was I thinking?! That was the worst idea ever.

Of course, all of this became clear to me after the fact. How often is this the case for all of us?

In taking my own advice from *This Thing Called Home*, I made a plan and I worked my plan. I was completely overconfident at this point.

Meanwhile, the kids were eating boxes of McDonald's fast food. When we first bought that home, our realtor said, "Brooke. Trust me. You're going to *love* having a McDonald's on the corner."

I smiled and nodded but thought, "Oh no, my kids don't eat that junk."

Well, in the month of survival, I was on a first-name basis with the employees at McDonald's.

In the midst of my struggles to balance, the kids busied themselves with coloring on cardboard boxes, eating Happy Meals, and running around outside in the warm spring weather. One day in particular, Scott cut up cardboard pieces and duct taped the "coolest fort ever." Our oldest girls even begged to have a sleepover in the fort. "Sure!"

I wouldn't have known to do this, but a wise friend told me to have the kids pack their own toys in boxes and tape them closed. "This helps them process the temporary separation from their favorite items," she said. I took her advice. Scribbled on the side of boxes in child's handwriting read, "Sophia's favorite toys," and "Save for Sophia," and "Bella's stuff. No peeking". And of course, there were many boxes with scribbles from little brother and baby sister.

I'm certain their adaptability and joy was grounding me as I was busy over-analyzing, planning, plotting, and balancing. At the core, I do believe children are deeply adaptable and mostly mimic the emotion they feel from their parents. Thankfully, my naïve, uncomfortable mental state belonged solely to me.

With the house still wreaking of fast food and old Starbucks cups, I landed on this one plan. I planned for us to sleep at my mom's house for a few days post-move before our long road trip to the first stop on the summer sabbatical adventure. Here's how I envisioned the plan playing out on paper.

Day 1 – pack all day
Day 2 – pack all day, finish 100% of the laundry
Day 3 – pack suitcases, live out of suitcases, pack everything else
Day 4 – clean as much as I can, keep packing
Day 5 – pack, drop off suitcases at my parent's home (leaving out one pair of clothes for morning)
Day 6 – movers arrive 7 a.m. and work until done, sleep at parents
Day 7 – rest, sleep at parents
Day 8 – rest, clean out the van, pack the van for the road trip
Day 9 – get on the road to Washington for the sabbatical
Day 10 – stay sane?

My parents were on vacation and their house was empty. The day before the move, I delivered our suitcases and an overnight bag with everyone's essential toiletries, a pair of pajamas for each family member, and any "I can't sleep without this" items. I didn't want it accidentally packed on the truck, lost, or forgotten. Nobody wants to deal with lost stuffies and blankies when putting toddlers to bed. It's like negotiating with terrorists. Not. A. Good. Idea.

This was a good plan. The only problem was that, again, I didn't know what I didn't know. Therefore, this shifting plan became a fizzling plan.

❧ HOW I STOPPED JUDGING ME

How many times does a fizzling plan happen in life? A billion.

And I know I'm not alone.

But internally, it was upsetting. I was having an internal fit that sounded like:

Why did I .... ?

Why didn't I .... ?

What should I have .... ?

However, it wasn't time to learn or to ask questions. It was <u>time to keep moving forward</u>. I'm the biggest fan of helpful questions, but sometimes questions are paralysis.

→ *always*

My parents lived about 20 minutes away from the house we were selling. The kids were across town, 25 minutes in an opposite direction. After 12 hours of moving, I still had my work cut out for me. Why? Clearly, I'm a hoarder.

At the end of a move, we all get to that point when we think, *"I'm almost there. Wait, am I? Why is everything multiplying? I thought I already packed that! "*

The delirium arrives. We're not sure if there's an end in sight. I'm not exaggerating. We had a big house and did a good job of filling it.

I thought I was a minimalist. I thought I was organized. Am I a fraud?

These thoughts kept popping up like a whack-a-mole game and I kept hammering them down. "Go away, bad and overly-critical thoughts. Be present. Keep going." I pepped-talked right back to myself.

I've always been a thinker by nature. I've always understood that, for me, a thought wasn't just a single sentence. It was a spark that lit fireworks, one after another.

One of the most powerful ways thinking impacted my life was in the day-to-day management of positive or negative thoughts. Did I always combat the negativity right away? No. I suppose I gradually put more effort into understanding my relationship with myself. It was part maturity, part learning, part just making sense of how short and precious life is and not wanting to waste it on over-thinking myself into and out of everything. So I learned to take a deep breath, believe in myself, and move forward. And that's just what I did in the middle of my parents' house.

It was my kids' bedtime and they were fading fast. Scott was over it and I was, by default, *going to get this move done if it's the last thing I do!* Scott joined the kids at my sister-in-law's house and got them settled. But the overnight bag was 45 minutes across town. And they had no vehicle. My plan was dissolving before my eyes.

I'm a self-proclaimed home-order expert and author and this is really happening in the most disorderly fashion.

My sister-in-law, Cristina, received me—sweating, wide-eyed with panic, and apologizing for dumping my family with nothing—with such incredible grace.

"Don't worry about anything. I'll take care of it."

I would do this for any of my friends or family. It just feels different to receive.

It was a beautiful example of extravagant kindness to me. She wasn't judging me the way I was judging me. She wasn't judging me at all.

I was. This moment changed me. Nobody was imagining the worst about me. I was being hard on myself.

❧ HEAVY AND LIGHT

All the weight I was putting on the-worst-move-ever had to stop. It needed to be light again. Failed plans and self-loathing were too heavy to bear. I had to observe and shift as the parts shifted. I couldn't do that with the weight of my questioning, or shall we say, insecurities. I just couldn't.

Here's what heavy sounds like:

HEAVY	VS	LIGHT
This is a huge undertaking.		This may take extra time and effort.
This is the hardest thing I've ever done.		This is testing my strength and perseverance.
I don't know if I can accomplish this.		I will work at it until it is complete.
I can't do this alone.		I will give this my best effort and ask for help.
It's too difficult.		I can apply all of my skills to this.
I can't.		I will have a good attitude and try.
What does this say about me?		I am enough.
I just don't know what to do now.		I will be patient until I understand more.

I have a friend who advocates saying, "Maybe someday I will be able to," rather than, "I can't." I love how she emphasizes timing instead of the finality of assessing our own ability.

Is there something you say you can't do? When you say this, what do you really mean by it? What if you could expand your thinking to *maybe*? I'm not talking about saying you can't because you're afraid. I'm talking about the unwillingness to attempt or determine a *maybe* rather than close the door completely.

My heavy questioning was just a narrative I was telling myself. In general, it was full of judgement. It had to stop.

I literally made myself stop over-thinking and judging *me*. After all, these thoughts and feelings were a product of my choosing, and my choices weren't working. I knew about changing the narrative. The basis for that is comprised of choices and personal responsibility. It means letting go of what I can't control, realizing what I can, and taking responsibility for myself.

Stop.
Breathe.
Think.
Decide.

What do I have control over? My thoughts. My actions. My emotions. That's it. Sorry it sounds oversimplified, but the truth is that I only control myself and absolutely nothing else.

No one was judging me but me. My choices matter and I could make a different choice. I chose to judge myself harshly. But I could start making a different choice right in that moment.

In meeting me where I was, filling in all my gaps, my sister-in-law's simple kindness changed me. I wanted to have it all together. I wanted to serve and not be served. But I had needs. I had failed plans. I knew I wasn't a failure, but I was at the end of me, and I needed something to give.

Cristina borrowed diapers, a bottle, and anything else she needed from a neighbor. She had hot food prepared in the crockpot and stretched it out to feed my family. She made pallets on the floor for the kids. She may have given my husband a stiff drink and sent him to a bath and bed.

As I received these updates via text, I breathed more freely. My chest loosened. I felt the color return to my face. As I drove back to the unfinished, partially-moved house, I started to make different choices. Moment by moment, tear by tear, snot wipe by snot wipe. I received love and grace from my sister-in-law and simultaneously ceased judging myself. It was time to keep moving forward.

In the past, I was the insecure mom who had a hard time asking for help. I don't think I always pretended to have it together when I didn't. I actually worked hard to have it together, even if it meant I was tired and alone.

But in these hard times, accepting help when it's offered frees us to focus on our priorities. Whether it's a large task that requires many hands, or simply a tired mom who needs space to breathe, we all need help.

Because I'm a helper by nature, I love helping others. The downside of this is that weird place where I feel indebted or enslaved to pay someone back when I know I can't. For me to keep moving forward, accepting help in this moment was the most peaceful thing that could've happened. I began to have the strength to keep going.

When you pass through the valley of the shadow of death, author and speaker Kris Valloton[3] says, keep going, because you're just passing through. Don't pitch a tent or build a house in the valley. Keep passing through. It's a season, not a lifestyle.

At the eleventh hour, I'll keep moving forward. This too shall pass.

I pulled in the driveway and threw the car into park. All around me the street was dark. Our neighbors' lights were out and I was certain my bustling would wake someone. My trash pile at the end of the driveway was despicable.

It was time to keep moving forward. I opened the front door and turned on the lights. My eyes beheld a huge pile of junk. In all the chaos, I forgot about my pile of Goodwill donations.

"Siri, how late is Goodwill open tonight?"

The house still smelled of fast food. The fridge was full of crummy leftovers and half-used bottles of ketchup. As I took out the trash, I opened the windows, happy to let in some fresh spring air and clean for the final time. I don't know where my second wind (or maybe third or fourth at this point) came from, but I didn't even watch the clock.

I zipped about my emptying house. I cleaned out the refrigerator, wiped the nooks and crannies, packed my husband's suitcase for the trip because he ran out of time, and took a massive load to a donation site down the street. These tasks took a really long time. It was hard and sweaty and exhausting.

Keep going, Brooke. Keep going.

When I finally looked at a clock, it was after 3 a.m. I hit the ground running at sun up and now here I stood.

Empty house.

Tasks complete.

Levels and levels beyond exhaustion. 100% tired.

I probably accomplished more in those hours at home alone than I did all day as I tried to care for my kids, field questions from the movers, pack quickly, clean up, feed all of us, and give the little ones naps. It was truly a juggling act.

I had nothing left but a warm floor. The moving company finished at 9 p.m. and the rest of it fell on me.

So I did what any exhausted mother would do. I collapsed on the floor and wept. I said goodbye to the past. I said goodbye to the feelings of judgement, inadequacy, and failure. And at some point, I fell asleep.

Homeless in my own home, I mourned my failed plans, my self-judgment, and my fears about our uncertain future. Shelter but nothing and no-thing. Not a towel for a shower. Not a bar of soap. Not a cup for water.

It was 100% unplanned, but 100% a present. A failed-plan gift, packaged in learning what I needed to learn instead of another pat on the back (which I clearly did not need). It was a circumstance that helped me let go.

I found a bit of comfort in knowing that in a matter of days we would get on the road to Washington and enjoy an extended family vacation. I knew deep down there would be sigh of relief the moment we made it to the start of the sabbatical. Yet, the looming uncertainty was composed of layers of questions. I wondered what kind of job Scott would take next, where that might lead our family, if we'd ever come back to Texas. I'm glad I had the wisdom to remind myself that we would figure this out later. Getting through the move was enough for one day.

The worst-move-ever was just going to be a memory of that one time I had an opportunity to be fine with what *was* instead of what *should have been*. And when the sun came up, the whole day would already be gone.

Keep moving forward, Brooke. Keep moving forward.

No matter what, keep going.

STILL LEARNING

CHAPTER TWO

....

Have you heard it said that you can't fail if you are learning?

I once asked an educator a big question. "Is it terrible that I never finished college?"

He said, "Oh, don't worry about that. Students don't go to school to learn. They go to learn how to be life-long learners. Are you learner now?"

I nodded.

"That's more important."

I was so pent-up on the certificate I didn't have, quitting this and quitting that, and my constant inferior internal dialogue, that I lost sight of what was most important. Lifelong learner. That is more important. Light bulb.

Even in all my failed plans, the worst-move-ever, and a helpful sister-in-law's kindness, there is the gift of learning. Learning is the anecdote to failing. You can never fail if you learn. The past is meant to teach. My friend Jeni always says, "The past is just for learning. It doesn't even exist anymore."

Once I changed my mind about my *capability* to learn, each day became a new *opportunity* to learn. Instead of possessing a paper that proved I learned something once, I was showing up daily, wanting to learn *something*: anything helpful, meaningful, applicable, or necessary.

I started testing myself with some big questions to see what kind of learning I was doing.

1. When _____ happened, what did I learn?
2. What would I do differently next time?
3. What would I do the same?
4. What resources can I access to improve the outcome?
5. Who can mentor me in this area? What questions do I have for him/her?

So, in processing my worst-move-ever, I walked myself through these steps:

1. When that move happened, what did I learn? I learned that a move is a really big undertaking. I learned that I should be more gentle with how I prepare myself and my family for a move. I learned that I tend to judge myself harshly. I learned that kids and packing are a conflicting combination.

2. Next time, I would ask for help. I wouldn't feel guilty for asking for the help I need.

3. I would pack an overnight bag and a suitcase for the first few days after the move. It kept all the necessities in one easy spot. I would also schedule the move a few days before we closed on the house so I could go back, make sure it was clean, make sure I didn't forget anything, and leave a gift basket. I was glad I did that. I was also glad that I took the kids to see the house empty and to say goodbye.

4. It's probably worth hiring packers, not just loaders/movers.

5. My mother-in-law has moved more than I have and could offer advice. I'd ask: when did you start packing? How long did it take? Did you organize it by room or item or just put what fit in boxes? Did you do an "open first box"? If so, what did you put in that?

I adapted to a different perspective on learning, personal growth, and what mattered the most. Becoming a learner in life changed everything. Circumstances are nothing and perspective is everything. I wished I was a student, but I was a homeschooling mom and homemaker.

Rather than sulking in that disappointment of what I didn't accomplish before this stage of life, I just decided who I was now. I was a learner, in the past and in the present. If I could harness that and reapply it, I would get back to what makes me the happiest: learning and growing. The other side of failing.

﹖ SELF-DIRECTED LEARNING

It wasn't long until I realized that self-directed learning would be one of my most valuable skills as an adult, not just as a mother. It's not that a degree or certification isn't valuable, it certainly is, but the internal craving to set goals, plan, learn, prove what I know, and reflect was a *real* cycle of a mature, self-directed learner. These abilities need to be applied to every situation and that was within my reach.

I hope I can encourage you to be a self-directed learner <u>right where you are</u> as a mom and wife, or at any stage of womanhood. What do you need to be learning that you could take you further?

Here's the definition.   *come as you are — but don't stay there!*

Self-directed (adjective)
(of an emotion, statement, or activity) directed at oneself.
"she grimaces with a bitter self-directed humor"
(of an activity) under one's own control. "self-directed learning"

(of a person) showing initiative and the ability to organize oneself.[4]

This was a skill I cultivated. It didn't come naturally to me. I was a busy mom with a fixed mindset and I moved myself into a growth mindset. I lacked initiative and always thought I was failing. When I saw other moms at home getting things done, self-directed learning answered my objection that I was incapable of doing the same.

Was it an ability that came naturally? Some have it and others don't?

No, it is mere self-direction, cultivated skills.

The very definition of words like *initiative* and *self-directed* are that if anyone can, it must mean everyone can. It further establishes the idea and theory that talent or lack of talent is a poor excuse for not living life well.

"The main purpose of education must now be to develop the skills of inquiry, and more importantly to go on acquiring new knowledge easily and skillfully the rest of his or her life," Johns Hopkins Education Department says[5]

Develop skills of inquiry. I read that and repeated it back to myself a thousand times.

I never thought of it that way. I began to wonder if stay-at-home moms, in the exhaustion and overwhelm, have lost the ability to be curious about what is happening at home, the environment, and the people and processes combined.

☙ LESSONS FROM SCIENCE CLASS

I have a friend who was a new mom. She was trying to embrace her season well. She was in tears often, confused and struggling to understand her role and its new responsibilities.

How does one swaddle a baby? Change a diaper? How often? How do I know if a baby is hungry, tired, gassy?

She had many questions. I could completely relate. As we talked it through, together we found an analogy to help her process her newfound role and expectations. "Everything I do doesn't work."

She had become fixed in her mindset.

She and her husband were acquaintances of ours and so, as we often do, we invited them both over for dinner. We ordered take-out and sat at the kitchen table fielding questions from these sweet new parents.

Some of the more shocking experiences a new mother endures relate to either sleeping or eating. How in the world do we all survive the astronomical amount of sleep deprivation new parents face?

I said, "Let's look at this like a science experiment."

Is there an uncontrollable outcome? Yes. But do we also make choices about the variables that may produce better or different results? Yes. It seems basic, but this analogy helped us come out of the trenches and overcome the feelings of inadequacy.

A basic scientific process is just asking questions and observing processes and results. It can't always be easily tested, but a good scientist carefully gathers, examines, and is willing to try different processes, repeat steps, or back up and troubleshoot. A certain tenacity follows the inquisitive and curious beginnings.

A science experiment looks like this:

1. Ask a question.
2. Do research.
3. Construct a hypothesis.
4. Test with an experiment.
5. Procedure working?
6. Analyze Data and Draw Conclusions.[6]

When you construct a hypothesis, you accept that what you do produces varying results.

Fill in the blank:

If (I do this) ...., then (this will happen) ....

This if/then model is something my friend and I began to implement in our ideas about nursing babies, sleep training, and other various parenting and homemaking concerns. What a remarkable feeling it was to step back and view it this way, as a learner! And by the way, her baby was eating better and sleeping better. And mine were, too.

Our emotions get in the way when solving problems at home. I replaced tearful, helpless sentiments (my house is messy, my kids aren't sleeping, my schedule is too full) with curiosity.

A fixed mindset can be crippling. We can get stuck, fixed in thinking things are just this way. A growth mindset propels us forward into learning and observing, realizing that nothing is so black-and-white. Anything can change, whether we initiate the change or not.

What questions can I ask, what can I observe?
Where should I troubleshoot?
How can I think about this differently?

I didn't fail to plan. I planned. But it was just a hypothesis to be tested. Something had to be observed, re-done, or asked in a different way. What a change of mindset for me! **Hard to accept.**

When I was struggling as a homemaker, I backed up and reimagined every problem at home as an experiment. Nothing was truly controlled, but everything was subject to adaptation to maximize my results. This was all fueled by curiosity instead of discouragement.

Before I began my journey as a homeschooling mom, my girls went to public school. And it was a wonderful season of routine for our family. It gave me the time to enjoy my toddler and newborn at home. And let's be real, having only two children under foot when you usually have four splits the workload in half, which feels glorious. And if you can squeeze in a nap before navigating that long school pick-up line, you're winning.

I did feel a little stuck when I realized the sheer amount of paper-work kids bring home from school. I felt it piling up in the kitchen and driving me bananas. One day, I simply had enough. I scoured the internet for ideas to corral kids' school papers. I was enamored by moms who just chose a few things to keep and threw away the rest. "There's the solution!" I thought.

I purchased a binder for each girl's school work that was exception-ally cute and worth saving. I filled this binder with plastic sleeves and kept them in the kitchen where it felt natural to dump our things. At the end of each school day, when I emptied the folder, instead of stacking papers and later being frustrated at the pile, I simply saved 10%, tossed the rest, and stuffed the saved pieces in the binder.

The asking of questions, the wondering how things work and why, the willingness to see life from a different angle or shift a part that can move, being curious, and asking myself better questions is changing the way I do motherhood and home.

⠂ DREAD AS A TEACHER

We all deal with dread. *I'm dreading putting the laundry away.* This used to be me. I thought everyone dreaded putting the laundry away and I thought that was just part of life at home. *You mean, some people actually wash, dry, fold and put away? All in one day?!*

When I determined what I was dreading, I could go back and see what could shift in that area by having a curious little conversation with myself. I was a detective and problem-solver of sorts. This is what Johns Hopkins University calls the "skills of inquiry."

It sounds like this …

To self:
I dread putting the laundry away in the girls' shared closet.
Why ?
Because the clothes don't fit.

So you need to make more space, or buy a package of hangers, or get rid of some clothes?
Yes, precisely…let me look.

This girl definitely needs more hangers, but this girl also has too many clothes. They don't fit in the closet or drawers when they are all clean.

And now, friends, we are on our way to solving this problem!

Simply making sure the clothes fit in their spots is the reason why I was dreading putting the laundry away. This was a simple problem to be solved. A quick purge cleared room in the drawers and closets, and suddenly the laundry problem was resolved.

To self:
I dread cleaning out my messy car.
Why?
Because the kids are always bringing toys and snacks into the car.
So you need to keep trash bags handy for snack wrappers and get a bin for tidying car toys?
Yes, precisely.

Plastic grocery bags or a roll of small trash bags stuffed under the passenger seat have been a life-saver. I'm happy to report it actually works to circulate a trash bag in order to avoid the pile up of yucky food trash. Now, of course, you could avoid eating in the car. But for me, it's just part of a life on-the-go.

I tried using a bin in the car. Too much to walk over. So I keep an empty bin in the garage close to where I park. I hand it to the kids to gather anything that doesn't belong in the car and we carry it in to put away. It mostly works.

To self:
I dread finishing my next blog post.
Why?
Because writing while parenting is very distracting.
So you need to find a time to write when you're not so distracted, or work some-thing out so you can steal away when you need to?
Yes, precisely.

The dread is good information, not bad information, when I approach it with curiosity, as learner or scientist.

Questions That Solve Problems:

It might be waking up to dirty dishes or putting the laundry away or something else entirely. Whatever that is for you, it's probably just a problem waiting to be solved.

Even a tiny bit of curiosity helps you rewrite the story. Make something new by asking yourself better questions. This gets us to the other side of failing.

Three questions that can solve a problem:

1. What bugs me the most?
2. What's the one thing I want to be completed each day?
3. What am I avoiding, and what is that telling me?

I'm beginning to focus on listening well and asking helpful questions when I talk to other women. I hope it clarifies and guides us into solving our own problems. I don't know everything. I'm not the expert. You actually know more about your situation than I do, right?

So it sounds like this…

A mom came over to my house after a Home Order class I taught. She was a friend of a friend and was intrigued by some of the concepts I presented. She had a bunch of questions, so I invited her over to chat.

She told me about her struggles with her three kids under age five. I totally understood that stage. She confessed that she felt incredibly stressed all the time. Again, a common feeling, and something to which I can relate.

I asked her some questions about what she did in an average day. This was my way of discovering her stress points. It's amazing how far a little curiosity can take us.

She told me about what she was doing, hour by hour.

I asked, "What's your evening routine?"

She responded, "Make dinner, eat dinner together as a family, give the girls a bath, and then my husband puts them to bed. Then we relax, chill, and sometimes watch TV."

Sounds pretty standard.

"When do you do your dishes?" I asked.

"In the morning," she said.

"In the morning?" I probed. "As in the next morning?"

"Yes," she said.

"How is that working for you?" I genuinely asked.

"Well, I mean, it's actually really hard. I'm trying to make breakfast and get the girls ready for preschool. I keep working at it throughout the day."

"Have you considered doing your dishes after dinner?" I inquired. "It might be worth it to see if that helps you manage your stress throughout the day."

We talked a bit more and I tried to encourage her.

It wasn't but a few days later when she enthusiastically sent me a text.

"Brooke, I've been taking your advice. It has made my life so much less stressful. My husband even said I'm like a different person. I can't thank you enough. Doing my dishes at night helps me wake up so relieved! I had no idea the problem could be solved!"

It was just a simple physical act. A simple shift in her routine that was causing her to be a different person, the person she truly is. She became excited about life, ready to take on her day, beaming at the very idea that something could be better, different, less stressful.

These skills of inquisition position you to be a solver, a doer, a learner. Finally, I became a positive person instead of embracing self-condemnation.

As a way of approaching all the negatives I fed my mind, I began wondering if I actually *could* do the things I thought I couldn't...or if it required practice. Sounds silly, but it helped me tremendously.

CURIOUSLY, I NOW PRACTICE THE THINGS I NEED TO DO.

One time, I parked next to a van full of older women on my way into a local jewelry store. I was shopping for a special friend's birthday. I did my ninja-style strapping on of the baby carrier. I put my one-year-old on my back, strapped him in, grabbed my purse, and locked the car. It took probably two minutes flat.

The lady next to me looked over and said, "Whoa! How'd you do that so fast?"

I laughed. "I know, right? I actually practiced."

"You what?" they asked.

"Practiced!"

Internally, I had to celebrate these little practices that made life joyful. These were the curiosities that led me to practice efficiencies rather than complain that something wasn't working.

I had crafted a mental game out of making life smooth and efficient. If something seemed cumbersome or impossible, I'd work at it. After all, it was just logistics, an impossibility waiting to be made possible through my willingness to learn.

It's worth mentioning that this type of mindset wasn't my natural inclination. It's something I crafted, something I decided, something I thought would help me overcome my natural tendencies to complain, be overcome with overwhelm, and overreact.

I'm naturally a type-B person, and I'd always rather be sleeping, having alone time, thinking about something, or doing something quiet like reading. I never really need much social interaction. I'm the complete wrong personality for having lots of kids and managing moving parts. I'm much more inclined to focus on one thing at a time. I think motherhood has a way of shaking up every type of personality and lifestyle.

Cultivating an ability to adapt to change, which is an inevitable part of life, was ultimately the most helpful part of adjusting my natural personality to accommodate the early years of parenting. I love habits. I'm a systemic thinker. I love anything that doesn't change. Unfortunately, life is change. I had to accept that.

If you're highly unsure and less enthused about learning, practicing, or adapting, boy, do I relate! And I think that's why I have so much to share about my process from failing to thriving.

For the least enthused, try starting by getting to know yourself.

Sounds simple, but it's actually really complex.

Getting to know yourself might sound like:
If change doesn't excite me, what does?
What's my personality?
How does it help or hinder my mothering?
What frustrations do I bring to the table?
How do I like to practice something?
Am I open to learning something new?
If not, what's keeping me from learning?

Whether practicing comes naturally to you or not, curiosity is your ticket to getting unstuck.

❧ OVERCOMING "I CAN'T"

I know so many moms who are convinced they can't do certain things (and I'm in this with you).

"I can't strap the baby into the carrier by myself, so I can't go shopping with him."

"I can only use the stroller and now he doesn't want to stay there for very long."

Have you practiced?

One mom told me how terrified she was to take her kids to Disney World because she didn't know if they could handle such a long outing. I asked, "What if you practiced?"

We had a great conversation about taking the kids to the zoo and practicing staying out all day. I encouraged her to ask herself questions like:

Did I like what I packed in my diaper bag?
Did it work? What would I bring next time?
Did this kid or that kid like what they wore?
Were the shoes comfortable and good for walking?
Did it work to pack these snacks?
Did the baby fall asleep in the stroller? If not, what might I do to make him or her more comfortable next time?

I think this works really well for road trips, too. Practice small ones before embarking on a huge one. See where you can use the small opportunities to grow into the big ones.

We took a 16-hour practice road trip to St. Augustine, Florida to see Scott's parents before we drove 32 hours to Portland to visit his sister. It's just practice.

You can't control logistics. There will always be curve balls and changed plans. But you can position yourself to be curious as a means of being slightly more prepared or overcoming a fear. It's an underrated part of being responsible. It's an idea for a starting point or a way of thinking about a problem.

❧ CYCLES OF LEARNING

The self-directed learner embraces a cycle that looks like this:

- Set Goal
- Plan
- Learn
- Show what you know
- Reflect
- Then back to Set Goal[7]

It's circular and cyclical and is repeated at our own pace. These are simple skills required of every learner. This cycle is becoming more popular for educators as they realize that students will need self-directed learning skills for all of life, not just to pass tests.

That was a wake-up call for me. If this is being required of young kids at school, I should start taking more initiative for my goals, plans, and choices at home and in parenting them.

Slowly, I was harnessing these lessons to get myself over yet another "I'm failing" hump.

Note to self:
Even in my mess, how can I learn and grow? Even flowers grow in dirt— I can too.

MOST PLANS FAIL
CHAPTER THREE

....

As a lover of all things organized, orderly, planned, and prepared, I think I'm onto something.

Why do plans fail?

It can be a horrible feeling to watch plans unravel before your very eyes, especially if you are bent toward order and if you attach emotion to efficient plans. *Raising my hand here.*

It can be equally frustrating to "wing it" and realize later that it was not a situation that lent itself to spontaneity if you're a Type B, easy-going person.

✣ BACK TO THE MOVE

With an epic fail (I mean, *ahem*, learning opportunity) of a move behind me, we hopped on a plane for Washington state. Scott sold his company and we simultaneously sold our house. I know, a lot of change at once.

The original plan was to take a long road trip so that we could have our family minivan with us for the summer. We packed the van just two days after our big, terrible move. It was overflowing with everything we needed to survive for a summer in Washington state. Each kid had one medium-sized plastic bin of toys, their favorite "knick knacks" and such. Each kid had one suitcase with clothes and shoes. Scott and I each had a suitcase.

We took a travel filing box with our necessities: birth certificates, insurance paperwork, the title of the home, and a few current bills. We packed a bag of swim gear and beach towels, fishing poles, and recreational sports equipment.

I stepped back, gazing at the van sinking low with the weight of what we had left, and said, "What did I get myself into? No."

Sigh.

The van was packed. *Where were we going to sit? Was I up for this?*

This wasn't happening. I was burnt out on virtually no sleep, last-minute moving shenanigans, pushing through until it was finished, harnessing every ounce of courage, motivation, faith, strength, and perseverance I could muster.

I needed to rest. I needed actual sleep. I pushed myself so hard to complete everything that I got sick. I needed medicine and probably a pedicure, a massage, a spa day, a hot tub, a chef, and a nanny. Ok, maybe just medicine. But you get the point.

No part of me was ready for this 40-hour road trip. So, right then and there, I courageously said, "No."

No's don't mean you give up. No's can be a wise act of self-care.

Instead, we purchased one-way flights to Portland to stay with Scott's sister until our van arrived.

❧ ADAPTING

It didn't take much for me to realize that these failed plans stringed together were piling up in my mind like the kids' never-ending schoolwork on our kitchen counter. I was processing them as lingering disappointments, and that's where I began to rethink what it means to plan.

What is a plan? A plan is mostly an experiment, is it not? I reminded myself of the science experiment analogy and the skills of inquiry. An experiment, or plan, may turn out the way you think, but it may take a completely different direction. The notion that you shouldn't plan because of the uncontrollable factors is pure silliness. But to hold your plans to a standard of perfection is just as foolish.

If I'm the girl who convinced you to make effective plans and work those plans, I think I forgot to talk about what it feels like when that doesn't happen.

You crumble into a ball of insecurity and negative self-talk, potentially blaming others and acting out in frustration, anger, or disappointment. Sound familiar? What are the other choices?

First, I made progress when I constructed experimental plans that went from sounding like, "I'm amazing. I'm prepared and I planned and I'm winning at life!" to, "I might be on to something. This could work. I'm hopeful and prepared, so let's give this a try."

My grip on planning loosened.

I took a step back and personified my planning nature with a strong persuasive speech.

"Oh hey, Plans, listen up. You are fleeting. You are a false sense of security. I like you, but I won't trust you. I will be ready for anything, and today will be great. Not because I married you, perfect Plans, but because I'm choosing joy no matter the outcome. I have a willingness to adapt whether it's in advance, during, or after. I like you, but I might leave you. My hope is no longer in you."

Are you so committed to a plan that you simply cannot win your actual, daily life? Take a step back. What is this plan? It is just an experiment. It might be a path to a winning day or it might be the detour and lure you into a place you simply cannot go. Beware, friends.

You should plan. You should make preparations and provisions. But if you need to let it go for any number of reasons, don't hesitate! Let it go and let go of any shame, too.

Adapt without concern that you've failed. Be willing to learn and know that every plan is merely a starting point. Let go of well-loved plans because you can't fail if you are learning. Failure isn't a thing when you learn from everything you do. That's growing. That's life.

If your plans are rigid, consider if they're providing you with a false sense of security. Does your need for security or stability mask a need to be in control?

For me, this answer is always *yes*. The root of my insecurity during major life events always stems from my need to control outcomes, to feel like I'm doing a good job when I'm the one steering the ship.

Navigating uncertain and unstable times highlight the ugly things we don't want to see in ourselves. Whether we are moving from house to house, or changing jobs, or navigating changes in relationships, or simply watching our kids grow and change, a false sense of security can try to take over.

I'd like to say I have the ability to keep myself in check and to be sure I'm not desperately grasping for opportunities to feel secure and control my environment. But I don't always do this well.

"Seek criticism" is one of Seth Godin's[8] life mantras. When I first read this, it sounded excruciating. I'd much rather dote on the good things others say about me. I'd much rather focus on and highlight my strengths. But, in reality, he's correct. Others have an uncanny way of seeing what we can't.

A season that's already painful and disappointing feels like a season when you want words of affirmation. But what if what we actually need is a little criticism to point out what we're missing? Better yet, what if I could seek insight and advice from other people who know and love me?

My second oldest, Bella, left me a note on my bedside one night before bed that read, "Love you, Mom. Did the dishes for you. Xo- Bella"

I loved it. I melted into a puddle of mush. I took a picture and was sure to share it on social media, hoping for everyone to enjoy it as much as I did. I equally didn't mind the kind words about what a good mom I am.

The very next night, on the same index card, I found another note. "Cool it on the chores, Mom. You pushed us too much today. Love you though, Bella."

Ha! Ouch. But she was right. So what did I do with that note? I took a picture and posted it on Facebook and said, "Just in case you thought I was a perfect mom, today I was a slave-driver and my kid called me out."

I knocked on Bella's door and she wasn't quite sleeping. "Can I come in, sweetie?"

"Sure, Mom."

I sat on the edge of her bed and thanked her for letting me know how pushy I was being. I welcomed her feedback and apologized too.

"It's ok, Mom. It'll be better tomorrow." And she was right about that, too.

Seeking opportunity for growth and adventure is foundational in acknowledging and accepting that nothing is within my control. I had to learn this. Nothing is ever truly controllable. Knowing this deeply prepared me to shift my mindset from craving security to being secure regardless of my experiences or circumstances. Being at home or homeless. I'm at peace no matter what. Because we can all blow it no matter where we rest our head at night.

Troubleshoot the experiment. Go back and ask a different question. What's the priority now? What now? And what then?

And, to comfort you, know that today—this day—can coast without a plan projected into it whatsoever.

Maybe repeat a good idea for a plan on a different day, or maybe say goodbye to it forever because it didn't have good results. It will be fine.

How do we combat disappointment when our plans fail? Adaptability, curiosity, and a deep commitment to being a learner is how you win that battle. Most of the time.

EVERYTHING NEW
PART TWO

....

"You're not falling apart. You're falling into something different. It feels like the end but really it's a new beginning in disguise."
MIKE FOSTER[9]

... time to
unmask and
see that new
is good.

LIVING WITH LESS

CHAPTER FOUR

....

After the move, I was desperately trying to become a learner and work past what felt like more failure in my own life. I was grasping at pieces of my new self, letting go of some old ways and embracing a lot of new.

Thank goodness for therapy, because after this was all over, I needed it. Becoming a learner and implementing strategies helped me cope. But at the same time, I desperately wanted to avoid pain. One of the best encouragements someone gave me was, "It's just new. New things are supposed to feel weird and scary."

I love the phrase "supposed to." I clung to that because, while life was crumbling, it was supposed to feel odd. Rather than fight to make is less odd or to reframe into a positive learning experience, I let it be what it was supposed to feel like.

It was supposed to feel uncomfortable and the learning was supposed to be painful and hard. It's why, as humans, we resist change. We don't want the pain that comes along with the uprooting. We want growth and learning, but can it please come from our comfort zone? Sadly, it can't. It's why there are those of us who always do the cautious and careful things because we don't want to feel things we're supposed to feel. Hurt and pain grow and stretch us.

Yes, we can have a growth mindset that sets us up for success, but it won't help us avoid the negative emotions.

Are you in a season where everything is new? If so, it should bring you some comfort to know, in just a little while, if you can hang on, it will feel less new . The comfort you crave will return. The fear will lesson. The pain, if you lean into it, can teach you something. The hurt can actually heal places that weren't right in the first place. It's like breaking a bone so you can reset it.

Maybe change isn't the only good thing to which I was succumbing. Change is good. Pain is good. Uncertainty is good. Maybe all of it could be for my good if I was willing to step aside and let it work.

⚜ AFTER THE MOVE

Three days after the move, our flight landed in Portland hauling one suitcase per person. I watched our old black Samsonite roll across the baggage claim belt.

Did I pack right? Did I forget something? Am I sure I thought this through? Oh, well. It is what it is.

My one suitcase contained whatever fit. The rest was in storage across the country. Nothing like entering a minimalist lifestyle cold turkey.

Yes, we do have small kids. Four of them, to be exact. Kids do need a lot of stuff. But, they don't need near as much as we are accustomed to giving them. I had wondered about this for a long time.

I'm addicted to purging and organizing. I love it. An overhaul in my home, no matter how big or small, always left me feeling like superwoman. I love the tangible results. But in this case, we were purging because we were leaving our beloved home and beginning an adventure with an unknown conclusion. It just felt different in the face of my panic. What if we need this or that someday?

Minimalists must be at total peace with the "someday" obstacle and realize that someday never comes.

What if?
What if?
What if?

So often, that's where my worry was born. It wasn't productive or helpful. I was starting to annoy myself.

I coined a phrase that helped answer the "what if" question.

If .... **happens, I'll *deal* with it then.**

Getting stuck on "what if" means I project worry into an unknown future. Why would I do that? It keeps me from living in the present and I become obsessed with what I can't yet know.

"What ifs" are stealing my "right nows" and I hate it so much. I used, "I'll deal with then," to transition my brain from the heaviness of worry. It helped me process reality.

When I was packing for Washington, I did my best to consider a different climate. Texas was over 100 degrees and had been for nearly a month. But in Washington and Oregon, that was far from the case. I was about to be kicked in the gut, yet again, because of another one of my own slip ups. I never checked the Washington weather forecast, and instead packed like I was headed to Bermuda for 10 days.

So, when that suitcase came off the belt, this is what mine had in it:

- 2 dresses: one knee length, casual; and one maxi dress that could be dressed up
- 1 pair of jeans: because, even in the summer, who can live without jeans?
- 4 pairs of shorts: 1 black, 1 denim, 1 patterned
- 1 denim jacket: you know, the goes-with-everything jacket
- 1 black cardigan
- 2 long sleeve shirts: 1 dressy, 1 solid black cotton
- 6 short sleeve shirts
- 1 swimsuit and cover-up
- Some exercise clothes: a sweatshirt, a t-shirt, athletic shorts, athletic capris, solid black yoga pants, tennis shoes

- 1 pair of cognac wedges
- 1 pair of black Havianas flip-flops
- 1 casual sandals
- 1 fedora, tan with a black ribbon

The minute we got off the plane and walked outside, we were freezing. I didn't even have one pair of closed toe shoes. I was desperately trying to remember what jacket I brought, if any.

❧ A TAD MORE MINIMALISM

We landed in the Pacific Northwest and rented a furnished home in Washington on Lake Whatcom. Our van was sent up to Washington from Texas via a student-friend who let us pay her to take the road trip in our place. She and the van arrived with exactly what I felt we needed for our three-month sabbatical.

"Minimalism is the intentional promotion of what we most value, and the removal of anything that distracts from it," Joshua Becker says . I mean, this has to be the right thing. Right?

Certainly, Liam doesn't need four blankies. It's time to pick one, dude. The rest are just a distraction. You like this one the best anyway. So, that's the one that went to the Pacific Northwest.

This is the lifestyle I always loved and craved. Many times, minimalism applied to the playroom, my kitchen, or a kid's closet saved my motherhood. But there was nothing like this experience to really jump start an even more intense minimalism.

All of our belongings were in Texas, except what I brought in my suitcase and the van. I didn't know if I was doing it right or well. Thankfully, Scott repeatedly reminded me, "Won't you just go get what you need if you forgot it or didn't pack it?"

Oh yeah.

I put so much pressure on myself to do everything perfectly when, frankly, it didn't matter. Because at the end of our three-month sabbatical, we stayed in Washington for another three months.

The seasons changed drastically. We went from the heart of July in summer on the lake—swimsuits, fedoras, rompers, and Birkenstocks—to thirty-eight straight days of rain in September and October, plus another twenty-one days of 40 degree rain. We stayed through ice all the way into December, just before the first big snow.

So my summer lake-house suitcase failed me somewhere around August 22nd when the weather began to shift and we were only on week 8 of the first 12.

I sobbed. *I hated minimalism.* I wanted all of my stuff. I was done being an adventurer. I just wanted to go home. But where was home? And what was this deeply-rooted ache to belong to some place? There was no home.

During the first three months in Washington, we spent most of our days outside either on the boat or walking along giant rocks at the water's edge. We managed to make some memories fishing. We had to educate ourselves and the kids about water safety, basic operation of kayaks, paddle boats, and a big speedboat. The kids picked up quickly on the hand signals to give if they were on the tube and wanted our boat to go slower or faster.

Scott and I read many books, listened to podcasts, and were fairly intentional about areas of personal growth. Scott wanted to take better care of his health and body. I wanted to learn to rest and let go, to be more present.

The end of our planned time in Washington went by quickly. I don't remember deciding to stay longer, I just remember sort of running out of time to decide. Fortunately, we had some savings after years of living on a tight budget and saving for something like this sabbatical. So work wasn't a pressure. We knew this wouldn't last forever; it was just a season we didn't want to end.

During the second three months, the weather shifted drastically. It caused us to find other things to do rather than hang out by the water all day. We found a local children's museum and purchased a membership there. It was a really economical and fun daily outing for our kids.

With enduring so much rain day after day, we ventured into the local library. The first day we walked in, my older girls fell in love with the librarian. She was so kind and pretty, helpful too. She loved my girls and they formed a sweet friendship. We went as often as we could and checked out big stacks of books.

At this point, Scott and I felt a little drained with our parenting. We began looking for a good babysitting option. I grew weary of lesson planning and didn't want to ruin my kids. So I decided to hire some part-time help in a sweet college student who came to our rental house. She took over my homeschooling duties and was able to help for dates, too.

One of our favorite past-times, once the babysitter was in our life, was to frequent the local coffee shop Woods Coffee. Scott and I read a lot. He journaled, and I began writing this book. We enjoyed the quiet, and we were both focused on personal growth. This time away was a gift.

I survived my woes about minimalism, packing all the wrong things, and adapting to our spontaneous life choices. Our life was very sweet and simple. And, dare I say, Washington began to feel familiar and comfortable.

HOMELESS
CHAPTER FIVE

....

When we arrived in Washington on our spontaneous United Airlines plane having ditched (I mean, *delegated*) our summer road-trip, it was just after 1 a.m. Scott's sister, Michele, and her fiancé, Chad, gathered us from the airport in two vehicles, knowing the six of us and our stuff wouldn't fit in her little BMW. We met them, carrying kids in their pajamas off the plane, every hand overstuffed with blankies and kid backpacks and headphones sticking out of my pocket. I wore Liam in the Ergo, despite being 20 months old and 20 pounds. I cried when I saw them.

It just felt like home to see someone we loved and who would scoop up a kid, push a stroller, and wear a kid backpack down the escalator over to baggage claim. I was really grateful. And running a fever. And sad. I missed my home already. I didn't know if I wanted adventure.

The next day, when the jet lag started to dissipate, Michele brought me all kinds of medicine and water. Apparently, at some point, she, Scott, and Chad fed and cuddled the kids. We made it. What a sigh of relief.

We survived a traumatic move. We survived selling a business that was very much Scott's baby. We survived the exhaustion that is *change*. Except all that change was also accompanied by writing a book and supporting four kids. And sometimes anything plus four kids is too much.

I downed some of Michele's leftover medicine from the last time she had the flu. I was desperate. I moved out of extreme natural and homeopathic medicine and into survival.

Today, I'm just here, and I'm just me, and that's enough. This is just the right thing right now, making the best of my hope to simply survive.

Nothing else mattered.

After the medicine kicked in and I took a hot bath, I opened my laptop to plan where we would live for the next three months. I had been writing a book, and moving, and selling a business, so there wasn't time to actually plan the sabbatical.

What I didn't anticipate was that AirBnB would have nothing available, and VRBO would have only a few available days here and there. The town we were going to didn't really have hotels. All the apartments and condos required 6-12 month contracts.

Oops. What now?

I cried. In my sleep deprivation, I literally sobbed. I felt homeless, again. Just a few nights before, I slept on the floor of our house without a blanket, pillow, or cup for water. Not a towel or bar of soap. A dead phone and no charger. I felt that feeling again. Yes, we were safe. We were fed and had beds. But, we were just temporary guests in Scott's sister's home and I didn't know what to do next. There was no "changing the narrative" like before.

What do I do?
What's the next thing?

This was a favorite question of mine when I was on a roll cleaning my house, or even when I had an overwhelming day at home. I'd ask this question just to move from playtime to nap time or nap time to dinner-time. It would ground me when I felt stuck and didn't know what to do next. During chores, I even trained the kids to ask me, "*What's my next job?*" And then, after that was done, to ask again, "*What's my next job?*"

So, right now.

I had had two big homeless feelings in the last week and I didn't know what I was supposed to do next. If I was single and a vagabond, or a traveling musician, or a passionate, starving artist, feeling homeless might not matter. But we were a family, and not a small one. I was mom. I had little ones, four of them, who thrived on routine. I was the queen of routines. But I had no clarity on the next best thing.

I really didn't know what to do next. I tried every Google search I could imagine. All I kept hearing in my mind was: *homeless*. I wanted to get back on the plane, knock on the front door of our beloved home, and say, "Here's your money back. I need my house now."

Waves of grief crashed over me. Home was everything to me.

❧ NEW IDEAS MAKE A WAY

Is there anything I haven't thought of yet? What am I missing?

I prayed. I thought. I prayed and thought and questioned some more.

Then, the idea. Thank the Lord.

Where are houses? I mean, houses are for *sale*. I didn't want to buy yet. We weren't able or ready to make a decision like that.

But I wondered if any homeowners with vacant houses for sale might let us rent for three months or be willing to negotiate some sort of arrangement. But I didn't have furniture. My beautiful furniture was 1,984 miles away in a storage unit. "We can grab a few things we need at the Seattle Ikea or on Craigslist. It's ok. We'll make it work."

I pitched my new idea to Scott.

I wrote to realtors. I included personal information about my role as a home organizer and author, hoping this would prove my ability to keep a home clean and tidy. I even offered to show the home for the owners. I inserted a nice picture of the six of us. Then, I crossed my fingers and said all the prayers.

I sent the emails to the realtors. Nothing.

Nothing.

Refresh.

Still, nothing. Refresh.

What now?

I opted to let it go and wait and see. I mean, when you are homeless, hope goes a long way. Certainly, the world is full of helpers. I tell my kids to look for people helping. Maybe a helper would call or reply.

On this first day in Washington, I wasn't just physically sick, I was discouraged. I chose to go to bed that night with a slight sense of gratitude for being at Scott's sisters' home. Her guest room had beautiful white hotel bedding and was sparkling clean. The kids had places to sleep, too, and lots of cousins' toys to share.

I rested my head on the pillow, too exhausted to wash off my makeup. A few more tears fell, and I weakly hoped that my mascara wouldn't ruin her pillowcase. I already felt like a terrible house guest.

Goodnight, hope.

☙ MORNING

A realtor called early the next morning. He said he thought he had the perfect house for us. It was a vacation home of one of his clients, so it was furnished. It had often been used as an Air BnB listing. Of course, the price was at a premium, but maybe we could work something out. He was on vacation in France, so he wasn't around to meet us or help, but he'd taken a minute to step out of vacation-mode to see if he could help.

Oh, Chet. You are a helper, I'm so grateful. Just the effort spoke volumes to my discouraged heart.

Scott immediately called the homeowner. But the owner was Canadian, so phone calls don't work so well. Chet, the realtor, sent along her email address and we reached out.

There would be details to work out. It wasn't in the city we originally planned to stay. We saw the listing online. It was way too much for us, but we wanted to see it for ourselves. We thought it was the only open door, so we decided to knock it down before we walked away.

The house was 250 miles away. It would take us roughly four-and-a-half hours to drive there.

We drove through winding roads covered in moss and trees. We drove close to several steep drop offs. We were so unfamiliar with the terrain, it was so unlike Texas. Breathtaking. I soaked it all in and couldn't wait for the sabbatical to start.

We turned the corner and met the gravel driveway. Our eyes followed the driveway to the house. It was huge.

Is this for real?

"We'll take it!"

Those little ounces of hope propelled us forward and took us 250 miles north of Scott's sister's house. We moved in to a lakefront mansion, with acres and acres to explore and blackberries growing wild everywhere. I looked at those thorny blackberry bushes, growing so tangled and crazy, and thought, "That was a bit like us. Tangled and thorny, but wild and free."

Just like that, we went from homeless to home. The seemingly-perpetual lump in my throat was slowly dissolving.

☙ EVERYTHING NEW

We were just a stone's throw away from Canada. We were near the base of the Cascade Mountains and it was all so new. So very different from Texas, "the land of big sky," which is just a Texan's pretty phrase for flat. I traveled quite a bit when I was in high school and college, but I'd never been here. This was like nothing I had ever seen.

Bright, apple-red rocking chairs sat on the back porch. The plexi-glass-lined porch allowed us to savor the view in front of us. We sat there. Sat. And sat some more. And never wanted to leave.

In our old Suburban home, I memorized the potential dangers for the kids. Our backyard was prone to snakes and fire ants, and the front yard posed the normal threat of cars. But it was a cul-de-sac, so even that was manageable.

Here, everything was new. I had no sense memory for what the kids could do or not do. They could roam, but there was no trash service because of the bears. We weren't in Texas anymore.

There was a path etched out in dirt from the downstairs porch to the dock. Little steps made of slabs of wood stuck into the hill. The dock was brand new. I had been on a boat before, but again, not like this. The drop off stole my breath.

We had access to kayaks and paddle boats. We even decided to get a big boat for tubing and water sports. Scott loved it! We made a list of what we might need: life jackets, a big tube or two. The list was growing.

We scoured the internet to help us locate what stores were around us. There was a Costco! I was so relieved to find chain stores I rec-ognized. But Starbucks? We were so far from a Starbucks. My old house was down the street from Starbucks. I went everyday and on so many late nights and early mornings when a baby wouldn't sleep. I'd drive through Starbucks just as an excuse to drive around. The motion of the car always put my babies to sleep.

What would be my go-to now?

More than everything being new, everything was temporary. I knew that at some point, this would end, and we'd go through the process again.

We were 30 minutes from any civilization. I started to plan accordingly for when we went to town. We would stay and complete several errands at once. It felt like a big task. What's funny is that, over time, we'd drive it more than once a day just because. Our minds eventually adapted to the distance. It's amazing how experience can shift our perspective so quickly and profoundly.

KEEP IT SIMPLE
CHAPTER SIX

....

I can over-complicate things. I have a system or an idea, a strategy or a plan for nearly everything. But in general, is it as necessary as I once thought? Maybe not. For decades, moms were content with kids being clean and fed, yet here we are trying so hard to do and to be so much.

If you put your hard-earned doer status on the shelf for awhile, Brooke, you can just be.

At what point do I have nothing left to give? I'm tired or I've endured pain or change and I can't go one more day. During the hardest days, the simplest things were good enough. They really were, to my surprise.

It's not that it's an excuse, it's a spare tire. Just like coasting to the side of the road when you have a flat tire and putting on a spare, you need to know that the car of your motherhood and homemaking isn't going to run efficiently in all seasons of life. It just isn't.

When a flat tire happens, whether it was suddenly and you were caught off guard or it was a slow leaking of air over time, the reality is the same. A flat tire means this vehicle is done for a moment.

I think you need to have a plan, a spare tire, for the challenges. And I think it's simpler than you could imagine. I'd love to let you borrow my plan.

For days that your motherhood is broken, do this:

Keep the kids safe.
Keep the kids fed.
Keep yourself safe and fed.

That's it. Bam!

I used to have all of these fancy ideas about teaching myself to wake up early to be Supermom. I would eat, exercise, shower, have quiet time, get ready, take my long list of vitamins, and then start fixing breakfast for my family. It was like clockwork.

But when I encountered a challenge, I froze. I didn't know how to move forward. The thing that helped me most was having the alternate plan: safe and fed. I defaulted to this in a season that required it.

For decades, parents did "safe and fed" and didn't have all the pressures we have today. Most parents couldn't afford all the gadgets we have. I believe that parents didn't even think about the newest trend, idea, or strategy. They certainly didn't have the pressure to share what they were doing.

They weren't watching other people do so much more because there wasn't even the technology to watch. Instagram has turned us all into vloggers. Providing a constant live feed of our homes is actually pretty normal for Millennial moms. Dressing our children in coordinating outfits for a picture that entices and sells, taking video snippets of our day's highlights, or crafting a scene around playtime that is more like a movie set than real life has become the standard.

If this Instagrammable life has projected pressure into your days, maybe you should take a step back. Do a mothering day of "safe and fed" and be present.

I found that the days of yoga pants, no makeup, and paper plate picnics in the playroom were some of my kids most favorite days.

Do you know how unaware they are of the pressures you face? They have no idea. They are just kids. The greatest work of their lives is play. They don't always need fancy meals or matching outfits. They don't need chests of toys. They just need you. They aren't scrutinizing what they have if they're loved.

If you feel this cultural pressure, or if you have put pressure on yourself, ask:

1. Where's this coming from?
2. What's the worst that can happen if I don't do _____?
3. How can I eliminate distractions and simplify this moment?

A spare tire won't last forever. Eventually, it wears and the car breaks down entirely. Yoga pants aren't my normal style. But for the two months we were moving and traveling, when life was full of uncertainties, comfy clothes were my spare tire. My routines weren't eradicated, they were just broken. And it wasn't the right time to fix them. Not all seasons are for fixing and doing.

LESS, BUT NOT HOPELESS *important distinction*

I found so much hope in the concept of *less*: less outside expectation, less self-limitation, less self-judgement, less fear, less mental clutter.

During our stay in Washington, some dear long-time friends of ours, Paul and Renay, invited us to join them on a backpacking trek through Mt. Baker. This is something I had never done before. In fact, I'd only camped in a tent once in my life. When Paul began to gush about backpacking, his eyes lit up.

"Brooke, you get to sleep under the stars, swim in the lake, enjoy the quiet, and rest with no schedule."

Sure, all of that sounded fun. But what about scaling the mountain, living with only a few things from your backpack, not showering, bears, and all of that?

The reality was that I'm more of a "glam"ping vs. camping type. We don't have tents or gear or sleeping bags. And how do you even meal prep for four days on the side of a mountain with only the things in your pack? I rattled off my excuses and reasons, but Paul was pretty persistent. "We have extra backpacks and can borrow a tent from other friends. Renay can prep the meals if you help with the packing. We can totally do this."

Paul and Renay also have four kids, and he was right, our kids would think it was so fun. At this point, I started to warm up to the idea. After all, I was outnumbered. And I'm a number 9 Enneagram[10], the peacemaker, so I usually make peace by doing what others want. Naturally, I succumbed.

I turned to Pinterest for inspiration. How in the world would I pack all six of us in these big backpacks for four days? Renay was a backpacking pro. I leaned on her advice. Mind you, we decided this around the dinner table on a whim, and we planned to leave in less than 48 hours. Time to jump into all our preparations.

We packed each kid in a gallon ziplock bag: one pair of shorts, one pair of pants, a long-sleeved shirt, tank top, and underwear. Then we stuffed the ziplock bags into a pack. With eight small children, I'm certain separating labeled bags would help us keep each kid's belongings separate and easy to locate. The bag could also double as a laundry bag for the dirty clothes on the day we would leave.

We looked around and took stock: we had a pack for each person to wear, kids included. The kids carried their own sleeping bags and ziplock bags with necessities. We tried not to overload the kiddos, knowing a heavy pack would really be tough given they were all under the age of eight.

This is gross, but it works: we took one toothbrush for the whole family. We packed one bar of biodegradable soap for the 12 of us.

We had to cut weight anywhere we could. We had a water filter, a hammock, and three tents.

We started the trek early in the morning to beat the sun. We knew the heat would get to us, so we set our alarm for six and did our best to get the kids dressed and fed. We crossed our fingers, hoping we didn't forget anything.

Paul sat the kids down in a single line. He got down on his knees and looked up at the kids, telling them how hard this was going to be. He said that, in order to be safe, they had to listen. He explained that, at some points of our journey, they may have to put one foot in front of the other and lean against the side of the mountain.

We positioned Paul and Renay in front, all the kids in between, and Scott and I in the back. And just like that, one foot in front of the other, we started on our backpacking adventure. About half way through, we found a large shade tree. Paul helped the kids take off their backpacks and told them to rest in the shade. We gave them water and granola bars to share. We wanted to hydrate and rest, but not for too long. We had to keep going.

Once we came close to water, the hike turned rocky. Now, I'm not talking small stones. These were massive boulders. It was really hard. We grabbed kids' hands and had to be very cautious. At one point, Paul pulled Liam out of my backpack and carried him across where it was narrow and really dangerous while Scott waited with the kids. The men took them one at a time, reassuring them it was ok. I definitely held my breath, unable to look down.

The glaciers were melting in the summer heat, forming lakes. We wanted to stay overnight near one of these lakes so we could bathe and filter the fresh water.

Thankfully, our skilled friends knew this area well and were great guides. We all could've died. But I didn't think about that. I didn't have a choice but to put one foot in front of the other and to be an adult.

We arrived, threw off our packs, and collapsed in the grass, exhausted. The guys saw ice (yes, glacier ice) and thought it would be great to gather.

Renay and I started setting up our camp home. This tent could go here and that one over there. These bushes are perfect for hanging a clothesline. She found a perfect spot of flat land surrounded by brush that we called "the dressing room." We had all the girls change clothes in there and use the "restroom" over there.

We unrolled sleeping bags and put them in the tents. We piled the backpacks. It started to feel like home. I'm not sure what that feeling is, but we felt settled and at peace. We knew how to nurture our people right here in this spot.

After we got settled, we all went for a short hike up the hill to the massive, clear lake. We washed off the dirt and sweat from the day's hard work.

We didn't bother to pack bathing suits. There was no way extra things would fit in our packs. So we undressed kids down to underwear and just started swimming, dunking, jumping, and the like. I hate to admit that I had to think about it, but I had been a conservative Christian girl my whole life. Never once had I worn a two-piece swimsuit. I felt so uncomfortable swimming in my sports bra and underwear. I had to really *make* myself do it. Then, once I was in the water, nobody was around and nobody cared. It was a funny moment of freedom for me.

The adults took turns in the hammock, listening to music and resting. We all filled in for each other, so whichever parent was resting wouldn't be bothered. As I swung in the hammock, I realized that my views on home had been limited. As a home blogger, a stay-at-home mom coach, and a home professional, I thought I knew everything about home. But making home in an unusual place or environment was foreign to me. I became a student once again.

Shockingly, this patch of grass and lake actually felt like home. We had everything in its place. The kids were either collecting sticks, throwing rocks, acting out silly stories, giggling, maybe bickering a little, but mostly exploring. We weren't obsessed with decorating, cooking, cleaning, organizing, and doing "home" in the traditional sense of the word. Yet, rocking in that quiet hammock, I listened to the pure sounds of frogs and birds, water and trees. I was certainly loved by a few good people. I had never felt so at home, and it was absolutely nothing like I defined "home" in the past.

As bizarre as it sounds, we remade home within the community of our families, with only a few necessities in our possession. All of our needs were met. I didn't know how to fully process my previous definition of "home" as 3,000 square feet of suburban life, with its endless dishes and laundry and toys and clothes. What I realized is that each of us has a profound desire to belong. Having that need met means that home looks like a thousand different things for different people.

❧ HOME'S PRIVILEGE

Most of what I was conditioned to define as "home" is a rather exhausting socio-economic challenge. People experiencing financial hardship don't have to choose to be minimalists, their economic status demands it. Here I am, well-off, pretending to be practically homeless for a few fun days while on vacation, having these epiphanies and deep reflection. But even that is an element of privilege. Home is what I think it is because of where I've been and what I've owned.

I'm not saying it's bad to be a "home blogger" or to teach home organization like I did. But it only reaches women in my same demographic. I have to de-clutter the more I own because, let's face it, I've overspent and own too much because I can afford it. The cycle of accumulate and buy, de-clutter, donate and get rid of, then accumulate again is a cycle of privilege.

I was so sure I knew everything about home, but I wasn't sure I knew all there was to know about belonging. Thankfully, this single backpacking trip set me up for sabbatical success. Because after our six months in Washington, we still weren't fully ready to commit to a job or permanent residence.

Truth be told, we flew back to Texas because it seemed like the right thing to do. The Christmas holiday was fast approaching. We flew into Dallas and stayed with both my grandparents and my parents who were residing there. We had a nice Christmas. Two days after Christmas, all the festivities were over, and we found ourselves, once again, stuck. We booked a local hotel, hoping to buy a few days of clarity.

We were, at this moment, homeless. We were living in a simple hotel, still on a high from six months in Washington. Our stuff was in a storage unit down the street. I still had one suitcase of things and life was...odd.

Scott had many opportunities, but those needed time to pan out. Nothing felt certain.

I cried and prayed, cried and prayed some more. Homeless. Discouraged, displaced, confused. All I could do was make this tiny hotel room home. I held my kids and played with them. We went on walks and went to the grocery store for a few items to fill our small hotel fridge. We set up mock picnics on the hotel coffee table with paper plates. Cuddle more, play more, tuck little ones in for naps. Fold this blankie, put it in this drawer, hang up some clothes, make a pile of laundry, put the pile of laundry in a hotel bag for washing. Go get ice, fill little sippy cups with hotel ice and water. Refill with more ice water. Rinse the cups. Repeat.

After our time in the Pacific Northwest, with all its natural beauty, this tiny hotel room in Texas, surrounded by heaping piles of dead grass, was mortifying. I was desperately replaying the memories we left behind. The water, the mountains, the layers of moss that climbed the tree trunks, the bay and view of the San Juan Islands, the drive up to peek at Canada's coastline.

I was devastated the minute we moved in to that hotel room. The white walls, the cookie-cutter furniture, the sub-par food, and the basic bedding. I missed the apple-red rockers and view of the lake.

Yet, as I looked over at the kids playing sweetly, I began to ground myself with my own sense of gratitude. Grateful for kids to hold and hug, feed and nurture, no matter where we are. Grateful for the sabbatical and the freedom we enjoyed as a family. Grateful for lessons learned, for the fight to redefine home.

Previous definition of home:

Routines, systems, organization, decorating, laundry, dishes, cooking, and cleaning with and for my family.

New definition of home:
Anywhere. ✖

My life wasn't the same anymore, yet it was *all* the same. I'm still here with my people doing all of these things. Whether I'm here or there, I'm still here. Not knowing how long we would be in the hotel terrified me, but it also comforted me. I was doing all the same things. I completed all the mothering and homemaking tasks that I worked so hard to master, and I prayed to God that I would be an exceptional wife and mom. And while I had no idea what our future held or where we would live next, this *was* home.

My biggest struggle throughout this transition was a struggle with change. When my environment shifted, I had a choice. I could embrace the simplicity of being together no matter where we are or what is happening, or I could wallow in the uncertainty, feeling sorry for myself and worrying myself to death. It felt like pain, but really, it was growth. And growing things must change.

I was reminded that the simple practices I once held dear worked well here, too. I found comfort in resorting to a bedtime routine from our time in our old home. Dinner, bath, bedtime story, prayers, and lights out. This simple routine, practiced over time, felt second-nature.

I rested in how simple good things in life can be. I wasn't fixed, or shall I say, *fixated*, on the uncertainties looming. I was letting my growth mindset replace every hard moment with one of simple joy. And as I was replacing my negative self-talk, my kids had done some of their own replacing.

The day we arrived at the lake house in Washington, the owner prepared a gift basket for us. It included snacks, a bottle of wine, slippers, and soft, bright, and patterned fleece blankets, one for each of the kids. I thought this was the kindest gesture. In the sterile hotel room, I glanced over at my children, all snuggled together in bed, packed like sardines. They each were snuggling their blankets from the lake house. It surprised me to see them leaving behind remnants of our old life, just as I was.

Goodnight, hotel. Goodnight, new blankets, popcorn crumbs, memories, and reminders that all we need is right here in front of us.

HOME: A NEW DEFINITION
PART THREE

....

"It's okay to process the weight of changing things, and it's okay to
not be sure of what the coming months will bring. But may you
know that even here, you are much more than those things and
there is still room to come alive and thrive within the waiting."
MORGAN HARPER NICHOLS[11]

You don't have to survive — you can thrive and come alive, too.

HOME IS BLANK

CHAPTER SEVEN

....

Home is _____ .

If I asked you to fill in the blank, how would you describe home? What does home mean to you? I don't know what definition you are assigning to the word *home*; and let's face it, my definition has changed so much. I realize it's normal to come at this from different angles.

We don't see the world as it is, we see it as we are. We have a vantage point, a way of coming at it. We have perspective, experiences, influences, and, dare I say, influencers. All of that makes up a voice in our heads called *narrative*. Narrative is the story we tell ourselves, the meanings we assign to words and thoughts. Narrative informs the way we think and live.

A few weeks ago, I was speaking to a group of women. As a casual way of opening our time together, I asked, "What does home mean to you?"

It seemed like a good ice breaker, considering we were talking about home. "Go around and fill in the blank. Home is _____ ."

I asked the sweet ladies to share with the women around their table. After a bit, we'd come together and call out words.

I heard words like: chaos, mess, overwhelm, heartache, where my crazy toddler lives, that place where I get no sleep, where the dishes and laundry overflow, and so on. I fought tears. The sad reality is that, for so many of us, home implies seriously intense pressure. I wanted to reach in and lift that weight off their shoulders.

Is home a dirty word, a sad word, a word that holds all of the overwhelm and negativity? And I mention this at the risk of sounding insensitive. But the truth is, the word home can stir up bad memories of abuse, neglect, or hardship. For those women, it will be harder than I will ever know to remake home and fill in this blank with something positive.

Did you know that out of 85 million moms in America today, the number one thing moms tell themselves is that they're a failure? I had that accusation on repeat in my own head for 10 years. I just had no idea I was in such good company. Home measured my failures. Home was the saddest word. I've been there. I wanted to quit every single day, especially when I moved and messed it all up. I felt like a total failure. And it wasn't because of a poor upbringing, it was because I was drowning in comparison.

How do we move on from this definition?

Home can be peace. I know that now. I fought for that amidst all the adversity.

Home can be order. I know that now. I carved and chiseled away at the stuff that was weighing us down and ordered the few things we needed to live and be together.

Home can be joyous, life-giving, and full of love. Despite ever-changing locations, we always found ways to stir up the joy and gratitude that rested deep within our hearts.

But I had to be willing to humbly admit that what I thought I knew about home was actually fiction. What I thought I knew about myself was full of projections and misinterpretations.

Brené Brown[12] says, "The greatest stories may be the ones we tell ourselves, but beware, they're usually fiction."

You can apply grace to letting go of home, but don't let go to the point where you give up. Grace isn't given for you to allow your home to be chaotic. Grace enables you to do home well because you have an unlimited supply of creative solutions, strength, courage, joy, endurance, ability, and tenacity, all made available to you by a loving Father who is perfecting you. He needs your partnership and He can't do it without your openness. Of course, you will rest, care for yourself ,and love your spouse, but you won't throw home out the window, because grace doesn't leave us stuck. *Never stuck. He's there.*

If keeping home healthy and nurturing feels impossible, if using home as your primary tool to love your family feels impossible, may the God of breakthrough visit your home and make all the impossibilities bow.

Let us assign a new meaning to the word home that makes home matter again. Will it take grieving your own past? Or therapy, or help, or healing? Maybe that, too. Let's carry that out the way a wise woman would, with small acts of great, faithful love: maybe some dishes, laundry, organizing, wiping of little noses, late night breastfeeding, some cooking. You know the drill.

You may not know what home will be yet. That's ok. Start where you are. Even if where you are is in a hotel room, a room at a friend's house, squished into a tiny apartment, or a large dream home. Whether a home is borrowed, rented, owned or in a person beside you.

Home needs a definition. You are the only one who can fill that empty space. And you are the only one who can admit you have to rebuild from a rough childhood.

My big, empty space was previously filled with the place of home, the gloating of my home skills, the pretty things, the rooms and square footage, the short drive to Starbucks where they knew my name.

I confronted my definition and ripped it to shreds. Why did I define this so literally? I regretted it, because when all of that was stripped away, home wasn't any of those things. Home had a heartbeat. Home was where I belonged, and I belonged to these people.

Now, profound gratitude crashed over me like a wave. *Why didn't I see this before?* Well, yes, I was pretty busy de-cluttering 300 outfits and tidying hundreds of toys. Now, there just wasn't stuff to deal with. All this time was freed up and I was confronting myself.

I was so grateful for the undeniable privilege to be together. Marriage, our kids, all of it. I was so overcome. I knew my definition! It was completely different. Home is a heartbeat. When we belong to one another, we love being together; not because the feelings are always present, but because we chose one another and continue to choose connection.

SPACE TO CREATE

CHAPTER EIGHT

....

❧ BLACKBERRY PIE

One day in Washington, Sophia, our oldest daughter, told me she had hard work planned. For a nine year old, I was interested to hear about this work. She needed buckets. So we grabbed the car keys and drove 30 miles into town to buy buckets from the discount store. She figured she needed ten buckets. We bought about that many. I don't even remember counting or asking why. We pulled into the long gravel driveway to the sound of crashing waves along the shore line in the backyard. I had a moment.

I let her experience total freedom. She was fully engrossed in the work she was going to do and I knew nothing of it. I gave no input. I respected her work. I just adapted to her.

I watched her gather her buckets, disperse them among her siblings, and give the marching orders to collect berries. Off they went. Black and purple stains covered their fingers and faces from tasting. When the buckets were full enough, they marched triumphantly into the kitchen. It was time to make pie.

Sophia had never made pie before. But she seemed confident, so I went with it. She described the idea in great detail. I nodded and smiled so she knew I was right there with her. I didn't interject.

I watched her spoon washed berries into a large pot and simmer them down with honey, agave, and fresh lemon juice. She stirred. I watched her mix flour and butter and milk and salt. I watched her search for a recipe and check on her simmering berries on the stove top.

Two months before, I would have said, "You can't make pie, you don't know how. Here, you stir the berries. I'll make the pie crust." I'd want to control the process and predict a successful outcome. I was completely missing the mark.

My nine year old made a delicious blackberry pie, from start to finish. She found so much joy baking that she immediately made a second one. We invited our neighbor over for pie and tea, and we took the extra pie to another neighbor. I didn't plan any of it. This was freedom, and being present, and being together. It was precious and addicting.

I was letting our homeless lifestyle mold me into less of everything I used to be:

Less controlling   *Here,*
Less worrisome   *too,*
Less planned   *less is more.*
Less expectant

More respectful of the kids' work and play
More spontaneous
More adaptable
More free

Look at this life we had stepped into, away from pressures and routines and doing. I was so grateful to walk around to the other side of me and see just that: a different side of me.

❧ I CHOOSE

Have you ever faced incredible change or challenge and found yourself stuck? There were days in Washington I felt that weight. We had endured massive change and chose this path. While there was overwhelming gratitude and positivity, I recall feeling stuck. I don't know if I can pin-point anything specific that put me in that place, but I think I craved routine and decisions.

I come from a decade-long culture that offered me many decisions to make. All at once, when we arrived in Washington, I had nearly no decisions before me. We weren't in school or sports. We didn't have any commitments to any programs or opportunities. Beyond deciding how long we wanted to stay on the boat, there were no decisions.

In the beginning, this was freeing. Toward the middle of the sabbatical, it was uncomfortable. We wanted something to do or somebody to help. In a way, I found myself bored, as though the gift of the free time was actually a nuisance.

One day, a friend from Texas text me. She lamented about her daughter's upcoming birthday party and how she wished I was there to help with the décor. I was famous among my group of friends for my love of hospitality. And children's parties were a particular crafting phenomenon. I revealed my boredom when I jumped at the chance to help her. "Why don't I just make a few party crafts and mail them to you?" She was thrilled I was willing to do the projects.

I searched for the nearest craft store and, to my surprise, there were none to be found. I finally found one that would suffice. I drove nearly an hour and purchased all the supplies I needed. I spent a few days making paper flowers, gluing pieces together one by one. It gave me something to do. With only a few possessions in our care and no schedule demands, I welcomed a small project that gave me work and choices (albeit, the choices were whether to use pink or white card-stock for the *Happy Birthday* banner).

Perhaps I had so conditioned my mind to crave productivity that I didn't really know how to choose rest.

All we ever have is this moment and the choices we make. Life is happening all around us, shifting circumstances. Ultimately, nothing is within our control. So, what now?

People claim, "It's not what happens to you, it's what happens in you." I cultivated a relationship with myself in which I was more aware and committed to what was happening inside of me rather than all around me.

Moments of uncertainty, discouragement, and fear of the unknown would sweep across my mind. I decided I could interrupt those thoughts with gratitude, joy, excitement, and kindness. I am that chronically-discouraged human who resorts to negativity first. It was more apparent than ever that I wanted to retrain my brain to love this season of change with resounding gratitude in the midst of the uncertainty.

always something to be thankful for ..

WITH YOU

....

Eckhart Tolle says, "Welcome to the present moment. Here. Now. The only moment there ever is."

I thought I was doing a lot of that, of noticing the small things. I cherished 90% of waking up in the night to take care of my babies because I knew I would one day miss it. I cherished little feet that fit in my hand because I knew in a few weeks, those feet wouldn't be as little. I cherished playing blocks and dolls, reading books, and watching little expressions of joy. I knew it was so precious that I didn't want to merely survive.

But what I didn't realize is that life is always pulling at me—forward too far into the future or back too far into the past. What will they be when they grow up? There, I've gone too far. Why is she already so big, it happened so fast? And now, too far the other way. I didn't realize how much space in my brain wasn't as present as I once thought.

We would sit on the porch of the lake house, rocking back and forth in the red rocking chairs. I would think, "Today has no schedule. Is that ok?"

It was eye-opening to realize our days were just about becoming and being present together. We flowed in and out of these moments of being present. Yeah, that snippet of time after breakfast eventually became lunch. But I wasn't so focused on the next thing that I missed the right-now things.

We rocked back and forth, devoured books, talked for hours. We watched kids skip rocks and explored 14 acres and marveled at blackberry bushes. I didn't interrupt or interject or project routine. This was it. We were living in total freedom. No school, just teaching ourselves and one another.

"Most humans are never fully present in the now, because unconsciously they believe the next moment must be more important than this one. But then you miss your whole life, which is never not now," Tolle says.

I believed in plans, in scheduling my days, in streamlining my routines, and in creating flow. But, why? Had all of that led me to this place of heightened expectation and heightened disappointment? Freedom from even the best laid plans left all of this space for creativity and adventure. And we were so happy.

⚬ WHO AM I NOW?

The greatest juxtaposition we will face in motherhood is doing vs. being. We are more important than anything we will ever do. Being a whole person, healthy and able, is a full time job at times. We need to know when to hold no values other than just being together.

As a homeschooling mom, I hear a certain concern quite frequently: "I could never be with my kids all day." Early in my homeschooling career, I had one of these moments. I panicked. "Oh no. Can I handle always being together?" The lifestyle of being together is equally the best and worst thing, and those feelings collided.

I had to grapple with this same feeling in Washington. We had so much time. So many possibilities to embrace.

We aren't always conditioned to allow a season to be so undefined. Where do we live? What do we do? How long? What will this be like? Who will we be? Our whole life during the sabbatical was undefined.

No commitments. Yet oddly, there was no fear in it. We were a family. We were a collection of people willing to embrace this change and come out stronger. Because no matter what, we would be together.

And yes, it took all the stripping away of life as we knew it to bring us to this point. All the commitments (and over-commitments on my part), the schedules, and the pressures are a huge weight. What I needed in order to propel life forward into a new season was exactly all of this.

So much changed, and in it, I saw more than ever before how resistant to change I was. I thought I had opportunities to cultivate adaptability in my life, but this was like nothing else I ever experienced.

Who do I want to be? I asked myself this question on repeat. I loved our physical place of home so much. When it was stripped away and we were homeless, what was left bare was me.

I cried many tears, wondering how my motherhood would survive this season of change after change, disappointment, and uncertainty. What happened wasn't survival at all. I looked around and used my anti-survival-mode growth mindset I cultivated the previous year. Not to form rituals, routines, or systems; but rather to grow. Here. Now.

Brooke, bloom where you are planted.

During our season in northern Washington, our time traveling all over the state, being in a different places on the regular, and toting our little suitcases with us, I realized something profound. The deep realization of who I am was evident, no matter where I rested my head at night. I didn't, in fact, need a home. Home was in belonging to one another.

We spent nine days in the hotel after Christmas that year in Texas, trying to decide if we wanted to go back to Washington or stay in Texas. The hotel homeless was altogether different than the Washington adventure. The uncertainty was building. We had all of our things in storage. Home was, once again, nowhere.

Scott and I looked at one another knowingly. In all our possibilities and choices, the qualities we cultivated are what would remain our constant. While it was awkward at the grocery store when the cashier asked my kids where we lived, the world didn't fall apart.

"We're homeless," the kids said. To which I replied, "Oh, it's just a short season. We are safe and fed and together. The rest will work itself out."

Who did I want to be?

That question resounded from the first day of the worst-move-ever.

Who did I want to be?

Who will you be, Brooke?

Even in this freaking mess, who can you be right now?

Who made you? Who is still making you new?

❧ THE MISSING PIECE

It's time to tell you a story from the worst-move-ever that I've kept secret until now.

Four days before we moved out of our dream home, I received a text message from Danielle, a girl who used to babysit our kids. She was a babysitter-turned-friend, and we had known her for years. She had a traumatic upbringing. She is a wonderful person despite enduring major challenges.

When we were first getting to know her, she shared parts of her life story. Her mother was a drug addict who chose a lifestyle of living on the streets. They were homeless. A friend of her mother, "Auntie," raised her. And Auntie raised her right. She took care of Danielle's every need. She fed her, cared for her, and made her do her homework. Auntie gave her a stable home when her mom wasn't able to overcome her severe drug addictions. It wasn't perfect, but home wasn't a happy word for her.

That night, in the midst of my moving panic, Danielle text me in a far greater panic.

"Brooke, I'm so sorry to have to ask this. But I'm in a terrible situation with my apartment. I need a place to stay for a few days while I figure things out."

"Sure!" I responded immediately, then stopped to consider my haphazard surroundings. "Listen. Danielle. We are moving in four days. But, girl. Please come. We have a spare bedroom. My life is chaos. But, yes. I have a bed for you."

Danielle's stay was a blessing in disguise, as she jumped at the chance to help me and to help with the kids. After all, they knew her so well. She would help me in exchange for room and board for a few days. It was great.

In the meantime, Danielle was trying to determine her next step. But there was a looming fear hanging over her head. She has no choice other than joining her mom on the streets. Auntie had moved to New Mexico, far from Danielle's job at a local public school. And besides asking some friends for temporary landing spots, she had avoided homelessness her entire life. But in this moment, it was so close. Scary close.

I was terrified with her. Although I was about to experience having my own layers of "homeless" feelings, I was not in true jeopardy of living on the street, begging and struggling my way through addictions and financial misfortunes.

"It's going to be ok. You have a safe place. Stay with us through our moving day. The first night we are out of this house, we're going to sleep at my parents across town. They have an extra guest room. We'll be there for a few days and you can stay there, too. So, let's look at the calendar. How many days does this buy you?" We stared at the calendar for a few minutes. I wanted to do everything I could to help her before we left for Washington.

I blasted a status update on Facebook. "Any of my friends willing to exchange a guest room for some help around the house? Very temporary. A precious friend of mine is in need. She's respectful and tidy." I went through my contacts, texting everyone I could think of.

I cried. I didn't want to leave Texas until I knew I could help her secure a place. I know that homelessness is a devastating set-back for a kind, driven, well-adjusted college student who has come so far. My heart broke for her.

The night before we left, while my family slept at my sister-in-law's house, I stayed at the old house to deal with the mess left behind.

In the mess of my failed plans, I forgot that I told Danielle she could sleep at my mom's house that night. Danielle arrived at my mom's house, locked out and dumbfounded. We didn't show up. She waited forever, but realized something was wrong. She text me, "Are y'all almost here?"

My heart sank. I had to keep moving. She assumed we were done with the move. But in reality, my move was still consuming me, eating me alive. "Danielle. I'm so sorry. I'm stuck at the house finishing my move. The rest of the family ended up at my sister-in-law's in Fort Worth. Let's see…do you just want to come here? I have a roof and air conditioning. I don't have any beds, but there is one couch. You can have it."

She came, and together we finished cleaning the fridge and hauling loads to the curb. We packed a few more boxes, and I dealt with Scott's closet, too.

I eventually hit my limit, and I could no longer go on. I excused myself to my bedroom. I said goodnight to Danielle, and she slept on the lone couch in the living room. I played a familiar worship song from church. And as you might expect, the tears began to flow.

I lowered myself to the floor of my room and looked around as the memories flooded my mind. My room. Where I delivered my son via homebirth. Where my husband and I laughed and cried, binged Netflix, and cuddled kiddos. Where I spilled tea on the carpet and scrubbed it out. The big window with the best light in the house, the best backdrops for snapshots. The room for which we saved money to decorate. The master bedroom of my dreams.

But now there was nothing.

I used the last of my phone battery to play Bethel Music's "It is Well" on repeat. I needed comfort, but I also didn't want Danielle to hear me cry.

I sobbed until I fell asleep.

The next morning, I woke with the sun and drank from the bathroom faucet. It tasted weird. I desperately missed the toothbrush that was sitting in my bag at my mom's house.

When I walked out of my house, nothing was with me. I had nothing but the shirt on my back. I actually enjoyed how light that felt. All I really needed was a cup for water and my toothbrush, and maybe a bar of soap. All of that neediness was melting off of me. My desires for a simple life were being solidified right there.

The worst-move-ever was over. I sighed deeply with relief. My gut-wrenching grief, my disappointment, my pain, my failures, my self-judgement, and discomfort all lead me to massively redefine what I always thought about home.

It was horrible. It was beautiful. The feelings collided, as often they do in life. These were lessons I was thrilled to taste, but they were hard to swallow. **very hard.**

As I hugged Danielle that morning (reminding her not to smell my breath), and locked up behind us, she walked down the driveway and I drove in the opposite direction. Both of us had tears in our eyes. I had, in fact, secured her a temporary place to live.

Many people responded to my Facebook status. Danielle had somewhere to go. She had a list of names and phone numbers. She would go on to call and make her arrangements, to settle into a different house. **Look at the grace poured out for her!**

While this moment was the first of several moments in which I would feel homeless over the course of the next year, I saved a friend from true homelessness in the midst of it. How completely ironic.

I made the drive to my sister-in-law's house, leaving an empty house behind. I felt every feeling there was to feel. I came back to the questions that were burning in my mind during the final days of the move.

Who do I want to be? Who am I? Who can I be right now?

Though I was disoriented, *where are we going to live, to belong?*

Though I was discouraged, *I can't believe I survived this move.*

Though I was uncertain, *when will our life stabilize again?*

I had an opportunity to decide who I would be. Kind, generous, empathetic, resilient, courageous, and mostly, selfless. Even in our disorienting, discouraging, and uncertain lives, there are people who need us. They are hurting worse, they're situation more grave, their homelessness more legitimate than mine.

I never thought I needed the couch to myself that night. I really didn't. Even in my hopelessness, I still had an ounce of hope to offer someone else. I had never been so proud of myself. I didn't have to *decide* who I wanted to be, I was already mostly the person I always hoped to be. I was her. Assured of myself and the peace I could produce through it all, that's who I was.

I'd like to believe that Danielle's crisis at that exact moment wasn't an accident. I'd like to think that God knew I needed to be reminded of who I am, of how far I'd come. He knew I needed to enter my next season with this truth on my mind: we are not alone in our suffering. And what if parts of our suffering were meant for someone else at that exact moment?

What I gave Danielle was the most *home* I've ever given any house guest. I couldn't present her with pretty soaps, towels folded into flowers, mints on the pillow, and a tray on the crisp sheets like I'd want, like I'd taught many others to do in my hospitality lessons. What I gave her was the biggest feeling of home: a place to belong, a person to belong to. I gave her me.

This is where we end this story. Homeless. I hope that, in navigating your own challenges, you can remember what I had to learn the hard way: less house, more home. More of ourselves. Less place and things, more of us. Our whole hearts open. Open to face our failures and shortcomings, open to connect more deeply with those in our midst, open to travel and experience life, to make memories, even if it's new and scary. Wherever we go, we can make home. And it's not about the list of things you'll need to do that, it's about the position of your heart to belong. *The position of your life to become new.*

Do people process a sense of belonging when they meet me? Love? Acceptance? Kindness and safety? Because, if they do, I really believe I have learned to make home wherever I go.

The *where* of our lives—though hard, confusing, awkward, and uncomfortable at times—pales in comparison to *who* we become. I can be someone's home because, after all, home isn't a place. It's a heartbeat. Home is wherever I'm with you.

HOME IS WHEREVER I'M WITH YOU
CONCLUSION

....

I never knew what this phrase meant. I think I saw some "doting new mother holding her baby" meme with this penned below.

Home is wherever I'm with you?

When I'm with you at Target, that's not home. When I'm with you at the park, that's not home. When I'm with you at the grocery store, the mall, on a long drive or on a trip, I'm not home.

What does this really mean?

Well, there was this one time.... We sold a business and our home and didn't know what would happen next. We moved half-way across the country and bought a boat and our whole life turned upside down in an instant. Then we moved into a hotel, then an apartment, then eventually another home. Suddenly, I knew what these words meant.

I traveled all over the Pacific Northwest with my family in tow. We slept in eight different cities and also in Mt. Baker National Park. Everything was new. It was shockingly beautiful and grand and yet, I found myself longing for a sense of home. I craved adventures with each dawning day, until I didn't, and I just wanted *home*. But, home was a mystery for the first time in my life.

I thought I was an expert in home, but I found that home was everywhere and nowhere.

The mystery was strange and unfamiliar in every way. Even scary at times. We weren't planted or rooted. It wasn't what I ever expected. Sometimes our adventures included people we knew and other times not. We were true vagabonds.

When I longed for home, I could look deeply into Scott's hazel eyes, and all of a sudden I *was* home. We were together. Our family completely together at all times. Traveling, exploring, being curious, yes. But mostly just finding joy in being present. Not merely tolerating one another, but settled in the feeling that for now, this is home.

Walt Whitman[13] said, **"We were together, I forget the rest."**

Last year, I purchased this quote on a metal plaque. I remember sitting on the step in my entry way, staring at the plaque on the wall and thinking about what it means to be truly together. Listening, paying attention, relishing, appreciating, cherishing, considering... I think that's what it means.

In this season of raising small children, I can't imagine a better home to give them than one where we are together, whatever that looks like.

As our sabbatical came to a close, we entered full holiday mode. Preparing gifts, visiting relatives, baking, and cooking. But, as soon as the magic of Christmas fizzled, it was time to plant again. Only, we couldn't. We were wrecked by the lifestyle we experienced. In its fullness, we were better people for making togetherness the center of our world and saying, **"Home is a heartbeat."**

After those nine days in a hotel, we secured an apartment for 10 months back in Texas where we had lived for seven years. But we left a part of our hearts in the Pacific Northwest and we can't wait to go back for visits. Scott will begin a few projects locally that will allow him to be with us more than ever before. He helps shoulder the weight of parenting without compromising both of our needs to do meaningful work. For this lifestyle we formed, I'm unbelievably thankful.

I called Danielle the minute we returned to town. She came to the apartment when I was knee deep in boxes and she played with my kids all day. It was really nice to see her doing so well.

When we moved out of that apartment and into a home, I revisited my own advice in this book. I called my mother-in-law, the "moving expert," and asked her what I should do. I followed every piece of her advice. I asked for help from everybody and let them help me. I followed my own tips in the Bonus Content section. And you know what? I finally learned my lesson. The move was glorious (thanks in part to my mother-in-law, who flew in from out of town to shoulder the weight of it).

We're settled in this new home. I'm finding my rhythm. I do have little routines, but that's not what makes me most proud anymore.

I quit homeschooling. I did. And we enrolled the kids in school. I drove Sophia to her first day at the big middle school here in town. I told her, "Ok. Now I know you're so ready. I know you're so excited and happy and can't wait to get in there and start school. But just remember, if you feel a little scared, don't let it bother you. This is a new thing and new things are supposed to feel that way."

Of course, I cried when we pulled into the parking lot with that big Texas flag waving. She's 11, and she's been my right hand through these tumultuous years of transition. She's my firstborn, and she's so grown up. I was going to miss her.

I watched her go in and counted down the minutes until I picked her up. I found myself, though settled in my new home, walking my own kids through the newness of entering back into a school routine.

What I'm most proud of is not the way I prep the lunch boxes and organize the closets and backpacks. I most proud of the way I took everything hard I learned and poured that into our kids. As I watch them settle into a forever home and a new life, I tell them what I've told you here. Change is part of life. Change can be good.

I pick them up from school and they hop in the car. They see me as they wait on the curb with their teachers. I'm coming down the car line, a big sticker on my car marking which kids belong to me. But as I come close, their eyes light up.

They know they are safe and loved. They belong to me. They know it, and so do I.

This feeling? This is home.

ACKNOWLEDGEMENTS

....

I, simply, can't thank you enough.

Thank you…

To Scott, who walked this road with me. I'll follow you anywhere.

To our kids who learned to be resilient. Mommy's really proud of you for that.

To Olivia Spears, my editor. You cast such glorious vision for my work and lead with grace. I love the way you find my heart and pull it to the surface. Thank you so very much.

To Paul and Katrina Sirmon, my designers. I'm so grateful for your brand strategy, design, and formatting. And also, for listening to my rambling for (literally) hours.

To Katy Crumpton for the collaboration and friendship. But mostly the friendship. I'm so happy I have you for a friend.

To Lauren Sigala because of your incredible work ethic. You push harder than anyone I know in the best ways, and you do so with grace, kindness, and adaptability. Whatever it is, you handle it.

To Paul and Renay Fredette who inspired much of this text and lent me our collective memories for this book. Your friendship is priceless to us, and we love your home so much we often crave it.

To the entire DC family, our neighbors, who loved us deeply through a lot of change. I don't know how we ever lived without you. Thank you for every sacrifice of extravagant love.

To Danielle, who gave me permission to share pieces of her story. We're so glad you're part of our family.

To all our friends in Washington that shared sweet memories, we wouldn't trade it for the world.

To Michele and Cristina Sailer who watched me gloat and watched me crumble, thanks for being the best sisters-in-law.

To these women I adore: Kim Robbins, Katie McCombs, Marla Swandt, Dana Sellars, Tracey Brown, Erin Morgan, Brittany Davis, Tiffany Miller, Cheri Duckworth, and Cami Armstrong. You are all incredible, and you gave me the most beautiful gift of reading this draft in raw form. Thank you for your generosity and your wisdom.

P.S.
And to all the hurting mamas that will read this book, I hope you know you are loved. Even in this mess, you will grow. There's enough grace for you to come home to who you really are. I'm with you and for you. I've been there. You're not alone.

xo,

RJ

ABOUT THE AUTHOR

....

Brooke is a creative thinker, writer, artist, teacher, singer, gift-giver, and also… a shoelace-tier, a lunch-packer, and (thankfully) no longer a diaper-changer. She lived a real-life fairy tale when she married a handsome bachelor after dating for only one month and ten days (best spontaneous decision ever!).

Brooke is the very proud wife of Scott Sailer and mom to four kids: daughters Sophia, Isabella, and Brielle; and son, Liam. She went from watching HGTV for nearly eight hours a day to being a committed, driven super-mom and leader in her community. She is a passionate, empowering teacher. And a good friend.

She has mastered skillet tacos, home organization (on a good day), and losing her phone. Her favorite "real job" was at Starbucks. This "type-A wanna-be" is known among her peers as an expert in chalk artistry, gift wrapping, and party and wedding planning. Presently, she is a stay-at-home mom juggling all the things.

Brooke is addicted to TED talks and dinner parties. She enjoys the indoors, the occasional craft, and she doesn't mind leaving projects undone. Brooke is a graduate of Capital Area School for the Arts and studied Communication Arts at Gordon College in Wenham, Massachusetts. For the record, her true "claim to fame" is her good handwriting (or possibly over-posting on Instagram).

You're welcome to learn more at BrookeSailer.com. But truth be told, blogging isn't her favorite pastime. For all the day-to-day insight, funny stories, encouragement, and community, join her on Instagram @brooke_sailer.

Can't wait to be friends.

THE SAILER FAMILY

....

Scott Sailer is a great husband. He's a serial entrepreneur, creative thinker, decisive leader, and the most likable person. He loves interior design, fashion design, and, really, anything involving design. He is a self-described foodie. He plays a mean game of racquetball and loves being a discipleship-motivated business owner. Scott is slightly more outdoorsy than his wife and he loves his beautiful home state of Washington.

Sophia (11 years) - Sophia Lane has leadership skills. She studies classical music and loves literature. She's the smartest pre-teen we know and she loves to talk to adults. She's still learning to bake and dreams one day of owning her own bakery.

Isabella (9 years) - Isabella Kayt is the sweetest young lady. She spends most of her free time talking about fashion or humming a tune. She can always be found coloring or making something. She adores her little sister and brother and can't wait to be a mommy when she grows up. Her current obsession is Barbie everything.

Brielle (6 years) - Brielle Angelis must have a big funny bone. Her tiny little voice is always telling jokes, pulling pranks, and begging for toys (please stop). She's gotten really great at dressing herself and playing in Mommy's makeup.

Liam (4 years) - Liam Scott is obsessed with his daddy, all things sports, Batman, and food (all of it). He loves the outdoors and can be found sliding head first down any slide. He's our surprise bookend and truly completes the Sailer family. Also, Mommy is very, very happy that he goes potty on the potty now.

We hope to have you over for dinner soon.

I mean it!

END NOTES AND RESOURCES

....

1. Bob Goff, Twitter, August 17, 2018, https://twitter.com/bobgoff/status/1030482396360003584

2. Self Publishing School, https://self-publishingschool.com

3. Kris Valloton, Bethel Podcast, "Walking Through Pain," September 24, 2017, http://podcasts.ibethel.org/en/podcasts/walking-through-pain

4. Dictionary.com, definition of self-directed

5. Jarvis, Peter and Colin Griffin, Adults and Continuing Education: Major Themes in Education, pg 48, 2003, Routledge

6. Science Buddies, *Steps of the Scientific Method*, http://www.sciencebuddies.org/science-fair-projects/project_scientific_method.shtml

7. Cycle of Self-Directed Learning, https://iu08.instructure.com/courses/96/pages/be-the-director-introducing-the-self-directed-learning-cycledelete

8. Seth Godin, www.sethgodin.com

9. Mike Foster, Instagram, https://instagram.com/mikefoster2000

10. Enneagram Institute, https://www.enneagraminstitute.com

11. Morgan Harper Nichols, Instagram, https://instragram.com/morganharpernichols

12. Brené Brown, Oprah.com, http://www.oprah.com/omagazine/brene-brown-rising-strong-excerpt

13. Walt Whitman, adapted from "Once I Pass'd Through a Populous City," https://www.bartleby.com/142/26.html

BONUS CONTENT
BY BROOKE SAILER WITH KATY CRUMPTON

READY TO CHANGE
A THOUGHT-PROVOKING JOURNEY
FROM READING TO DOING

....

Hi new friends,

Are you ready to face your life as it is right now, but wondering what's next?

Now that you have read (We're) Home.less, I thought you might like a chance to dig a little deeper. Sometimes I get stuck because I don't know what to do next. While reading a book can help, we aren't always sure how to let those words influence our lives moving forward. I hope the resources you're about to encounter in this part of the book are your next steps.

This Bonus Content section is full of tips and tricks for navigating your own seasons of transition. But first, my friend Katy and I are asking you to sit with some thought-provoking questions. Let's get to the heart of the matter so you don't have to go around this mountain again. Because to be honest, after the fourth time we moved in the course of two years, I was floundering. I wished I had recorded what I learned the first time.

What questions should you be asking yourself? How do you discover what is really important to you in your individual experience and circumstance?

Feel free to follow along in the book and make notes.

I invited my friend, Katy, to co-write the journal with me. She's a precious mama to four boys and has tackled cross-country road trips and other big moves, too. She is a homeschooling mom. But more than all of that, she's the friend who offered to be my pen pal when our life turned upside down.

We wrote letters back and forth the entire time we ventured out to Washington for the sabbatical, when we stopped at an inn overnight, when I was at the lake house, and everywhere in between. Do you know what you need the most when life is so uncertain? A steady friend. Not advice or problem-solving techniques. Just a friend who is willing to walk the road with you, come what may. That's why I asked her to join our conversation.

This section starts with the journal, then moves to a lies vs. truth chart, tips for moving, tips for helping kids adjust to change, and more. I hope this helps set you on the right track.

Pretend I'm right beside you, nudging you along, ok? Making and remaking home is an ongoing process, and I'm in this with you, navigating my own messes.

You can find printable versions of these resources and ongoing conversations at brookesailer.com. And for those of you coming from a background of faith, I've created a 5-day devotional for you. It's complete with verses to meditate on and worship songs to listen to as you find your way in challenging times.

You can do this!

Brooke

JOURNAL PROMPTS

....

PART 1

....

If you are married or in a relationship, how does your partner see life differently than you? Do they yearn for the outdoors, enjoy visiting the same places on vacation every year, desire to stick to his roots, or adventure into the unknown?

_____

_____

_____

_____

_____

_____

_____

_____

How does that differ from you?

It's good to be aware of the full joy of your spouse in these moments because it helps show compassion for differences and celebrate similarities. Change is much easier with a partner.

What can you actually control?

Recall Brooke's traumatic move and the moments she compared to the valley of the shadow of death. What valleys have you traveled through in your own life? When have you had to talk yourself through something, big or small? Motherhood is so exhausting. I have had to talk myself through putting away laundry. But you get it done. And you move forward. Hard is not bad.

What would a "life-long learner" really look like to you?

When Brooke talked about changing her capability to learn, she started asking some big questions. Meditate on this for awhile.

Do you have a problem to solve? Do you want to do something better? Let's take an algorithmic approach and answer these questions. It might shed tons of light on your current circumstance (taken straight from Chapter 2).

1. When _____ happened, what did I learn?
2. What would I do differently next time?
3. What would I do the same?
4. What resources can I access to improve the outcome?
5. Who can mentor me in this area? What questions do I have for him/her?

Areas of life where things just aren't working:

1. ....

2. ....

3. ....

4. ....

5. ....

Write this down:

(Your Name) is a learner.

(Your Name) can solve problems.

(Your Name) can be ....

How? Think. Write out some ideas. If you don't know what will help turn the corner, write down who you can go to for help. That's a great first step!

....

....

....

....

....

....

....

Getting to know yourself (from Chapter 2):
1. If change doesn't excite me, what does?
2. What's my personality?
3. How does it help or hinder my mothering?
4. What frustrations do I bring to the table?
5. How do I like to practice something?
6. Am I open to learning something new?
7. If not, what's keeping me from learning?

What stands out to you about failed plans and learning? Write it down in your own words.

When plans go awry, what can you say to yourself that resonates with your spirit? Circle or write it in:

"It's ok…"   "Peace…"   "Let's reevaluate…"

"Adjust…"   "No biggie…"   "Take a breather…"

"I've got this…"   "No prob, Bob…"   _____

PART 2

....

Are there spaces or rooms in your home that would benefit from a little minimalism? A playroom? Closet? Bookshelf? Usually, we know exactly where it's needed.

_____

_____

_____

_____

_____

_____

_____

_____

_____

What are some strategies to get that task(s) done?

What's holding you back?

How does fear and scarcity tie you to your "things"?

Who in your life would unashamedly, without question, come to your aid in a time of trauma?

Who are the people in your life you would help in a time of trauma, without question?

....

....

....

....

....

....

....

....

Finish this sentence:

Home is ....

....

....

....

....

Brooke mentioned that when there is an unexpected obstacle, she had a default plan: keep the kids safe, keep the kids fed, keep yourself safe and fed. If you could summarize your most important precepts in a short phrase, what would it be? This can help you keep things moving when you feel stuck in the midst of change.

PART 3

....

What does living "in the now," in the present, mean to you?

_____

_____

_____

_____

_____

_____

_____

_____

_____

What would your day look like if you did actually live in the present moment (we're brainstorming here, there are no wrong answers)?

What would your heart look like, how would your spirit feel, if this was your reality?

Have there been moments in your life when you've experienced life like this? Maybe on summer break, a vacation, or maybe during the week after Christmas? If yes, what caused it to slip away? What let "life" back in?

What gifts do you embody, that are unique to you, that you can rely on, even when everything else is falling apart?

How has reading this narrative changed your definition of home?

❧ I'M COMMITTING ❧

I, ... , am ready to change.
(name)

I commit to a first step:

_____

_____

And a second step:

_____

_____

_____
(This Date)

I will commit to my first step.

_____
(Signature)

LIE VS. TRUTH
(REGARDING TRANSITIONS)

....

LIE	TRUTH
This uncertainty will never end.	It will. Life is full of ups and downs. Just because this season feels down doesn't mean things can't turn around on a moment's notice.
My disappointment is too big. My heart will ache over this for a long time.	Research shows that disappointments do take time to heal. It may take about a year, but your heart will find a way to beat again. Lean into the hurt and ask, "What can I learn from this?" While it's difficult, and others may not fully understand, try to remember that the past can't be changed. The future, however, is full of possibilities.
I'm alone.	When we feel discouraged, it's easy to forget that many people are willing to help and to extend kindness and generosity. You may experience loneliness, but you also have a choice to befriend someone who needs support just like you do.

Change is bad.	Change is hard. It's typically neither good or bad, but a mixture of both. As humans, we are creatures of habit, and many of us resist change. It takes time and effort to adjust. It can be uncomfortable and even painful, but that doesn't make it bad. Our attitudes and perspectives are a better indicator of the long-term outcome.
I can make new friends right away.	I have to be intentional and notice others around me. Often, I have to reach out to others and pursue friendship. I may have to take the first step, to invite a friend over for a play date or to meet up for coffee. Then, I'll have to be consistent. I'll need to show that I care. It takes time and effort.
I can unpack everything today.	Unpacking is a process. And it probably won't happen overnight. It's hard work, but small progress adds up. Take one box at a time. That's the best you can do. In fact, you'll probably leave a handful of boxes in the garage, attic, or corner of the room for some time. And that's ok.
I'll never find my way around this town.	Experts say it takes three years to fully adjust to new surroundings and for a new environment to become familiar. In the meantime, Google is useful. Knowing the basics helps a lot: locate grocery stores, the post office, gas stations, etc.

Lie	Truth
I'll get to this later.	Beware of excuses. Deal with the mess or box or suitcase now so you don't create more work for yourself later. "Touch it once" is a great rule of thumb if you tend to shuffle clutter without tackling it effectively. Sometimes, during transition, we give ourselves permission to put certain things off until later that are *actually* big priorities.
We're only here temporarily, it's not worth investing in friends.	Truth: Even on short vacations or sabbaticals, connection improves our lives exponentially. It can be uncomfortable to be friendly to a stranger, but you never know when that stranger can become a friend.

LIE	TRUTH

WHAT TO PACK
THREE THINGS TO PACK FOR YOUR KIDS
ON ANY LONG OR SHORT TRIP

....

- **Busy activities**—Coloring books and crayons, electronic device and headphones, a few favorite toys, etc.

- **Comfort items**—A stuffed animal, blankie, etc. Consider anything that your child loves, and especially loves for sleeping.

- **Snacks**—Everyone inevitably gets hungry before you arrive anywhere. My kids like protein bars, pretzels, applesauce, and crackers. If you can, pack a cooler and plan ahead for healthy meals. It saves money and meals will be more well-rounded.

Note for comfort items:
When Isabella was almost two years old, she was about to move into a big-girl bed and our family was about to move into a new home across town. It was a lot of new for a little one. She wasn't attached to any sort of comfort item, but I wanted her to be.

I began putting the same soft, plush doll in her bed with her at night. We talked to the doll, tucked the doll into bed, read to the doll, and role-played with the doll. I called the doll "baby."

"Here, hold your baby. Kiss your baby. Oh, I think your baby wants to sleep with you!"

After doing this consistently for a week, she began to want to cuddle and sleep with "baby." She woke up and asked if "baby" wanted scrambled eggs, too. "Baby" made trips to the grocery store, the park, or a doctor's appointment with us. Soon, "baby" earned her spot in the stroller next to Isabella.

I was thrilled. It may not be this simple for your child, but this gave Isabella great comfort when we moved from the apartment into our home. It gave her something to love and to nurture.

The simple consistency of having the doll with her at all times proved successful, because when Isabella was sad, nervous, scared, or simply upset, "baby" would give her comfort.

Ideas of what to pack:

TIPS FOR MOVING
TOP 3 TIPS FOR MOVING

....

1. Label a box "open first." Load it on the moving truck last so it's the first to come off the truck at your new location. The "open first" box needs: sheets, hardware for putting beds together, some tools for putting beds together, and bath towels.

2. Keep these items handy on the first day of moving in: box cutters, scissors, trash bags, toilet paper, cleaning supplies, paper towels, hand soap (in every bathroom and kitchen), paper plates, plastic utensils and cups, and dish towels. I loaded these items into a laundry basket and drove them in my own car to the new house so I wasn't searching for them on a moving truck.

3. Clear your calendar so that you have a few days to settle into a new home and clean your old home when it's empty. This margin will give you space to breathe. *Note: Unless you are a tried-and-true minimalist, everything takes longer than you imagine.* If you are signing closing papers, leave extra time to be certain your old home is empty, clear, and clean at least 24 hours before you sign. Just to be extra kind, I left a welcome basket for the new homeowners with bottles of water, a bag of snacks, a list of phone numbers of the businesses that serviced our home, and a note that said, "Welcome. Hope you love this home as much as we did and make beautiful memories." I also left our extra keys and the garage door opener.

A note on moving for moms with babies and toddlers:
If you have family members, babysitters, or close friends, take all the help you can get. As early as six weeks before you move, invite a babysitter over to play with the kids while you pack. Or send the kids for a sleepover at grandma or auntie's house.

Hire packers if you have a nursing baby or a toddler who desperately needs you. You won't have a lot of margin or focus on packing. Also, you could sleep at a friend's house on the day you move in so you don't have the pressure of getting beds put together on the day you unload the truck. Using a baby carrier can free your hands. If you have no help, kiddos might need a bit of screen time to occupy them. That's ok. You can introduce balance later.

Ideas for helping me have a successful move:

....

....

....

....

....

....

....

....

....

....

SETTLING KIDS
TIPS FOR SETTLING A WORRIED, FRIGHTENED, OR UNCERTAIN CHILD IN A NEW PLACE

....

During our time of transition, my children required increased levels of physical affection and positive affirmation in order to feel safe. Thankfully, a friend previously shared a psychology article that circulated social media, and I remember catching a glimpse of it. It mentioned increasing affection and positivity with kids in times of change. So this is what it looked like for us (fill in the blank spaces with additional ideas):

Physical affection looked like:

- Cuddling on the couch.
- Sitting on my lap for a book or movie.
- Hugs.
- Sweet pats or rubs on the back or shoulders.
- Holding hands.
- Holding, carrying, or rocking.
- Co-sleeping.

- ....

- ....

- ....

Positive things to say to your kids:

- I'm grateful for you.
- Thanks for _____. I really appreciate that.
- That was a great choice.
- I'm learning new things from you.
- You're so important to me.
- You did a good job.
- I love you.

- ....

- ....

- ....

How do my children settle down when they are unsure or upset?

....

....

....

....

....

....

....

....

....

....

PARENTING THROUGH CHANGE
LITTLE PREPARATIONS FOR BIG CHANGES

....

Friend, let's not pretend I knew what I was doing. I most certainly did not. But, looking back, I didn't do *everything* wrong. Sometimes my brain wants to trick me into thinking, "I did everything wrong," or, "I did everything right." In fact, I experienced a combination of both.

Extra intention here and there really did help us all. For example, I made the extra effort to take the kids to our old house when it was empty to let them see it before we left town (this was a tip from a friend.) I loved hearing their stories and favorite memories from our time in that house. This was one of those things that worked. Let me list out a few other ideas.

How to prepare your children for a big change:

- **Affirm that you can be trusted.**
  I knew we weren't just navigating a move. There were layers of uncertainty. I tried to listen for insecurities the kids might have and allow them to grow trust between us.

  "I know it's hard not knowing what job Daddy's going to have, but Mommy and Daddy will always take care of you."

- **Give space for appreciating and expressing past memories.**
  "We're going to visit our old house. I know it's going to look empty and different, but take a minute to look in your old room."

I actually made my kids say, "thank you and goodbye," Marie Kondo style. I know it's just an empty house and it's not a human, but sitting on the floor and remembering everything helps cultivate a little gratitude where you need it. I also took pictures so we could revisit them together when they were sad.

- **Involve kids in the process of packing and labeling their own boxes.**
  Granted, this was hard, because they would pack and then play, then unpack what they packed, and play some more. However, they had an easier time temporarily parting with items going in storage and enjoyed unpacking because they remembered where they put each item and recognized their own handwriting. I also used colored duct tape for each kid's boxes. "Pink tape goes to my room!" Brielle scanned the moving truck for the hot pink tape. It gave her something to look forward to.

Lastly, communication is key. My kids handled it well when I communicated what to expect. For example: "This is your backpack for the airplane. We're going to be sitting down for a really long time. You'll have to stay in your seat and it might feel long. But you can take a nap if you want. Let's pack your blankie." It helps later when, as the parent, you reinforce, "Please stay in your seat."

Expectation without communication never works. Your child doesn't know what to expect when they face something new. Clearly communicating instructions in a gentle tone went a long way.

Can you prepare your kids for everything? Nope! So hold these tips with an open hand and remember, as Katy said, "Kids are resilient."

HOME IS ...

....

How do I define my own home? Remember in Chapter Nine, we were reminded that home is *blank*? Words are simply thought capsules. The word *home* could mean a thousand different things. And, maybe, if you write it down, you'll capture the heartbeat behind your own home.

Circle these adjectives or add your own. The definition is up to you. You decide based on your values. Remember, there's no wrong answer!

Home is:

Kind	Empathetic	Generous
Safe	Peaceful	A Refuge
Comfort	Loving	Exciting
Loud	Quiet	Playful

Full of Memories

....

"Home, after all, isn't a place. It's a heartbeat."
BROOKE SAILER

WHO I WANT TO BE

....

No matter where you are, the person you are becoming is far more import-ant. Though I found myself stuck in an in-between season of life, living in a hotel, I had to decide who I wanted to be. Yes, many personality traits are innate and will come naturally to you. However, many good qualities will be attributes you choose to cultivate. Whether you live in a small home, a large home, a trailer, a renovated tiny home on wheels or you share an apartment with roommates, you can be the best version of yourself.

No matter where I am, this is who I want to be:
(Circle the attributes you'd like to cultivate or believe you already have. Then, add in your own thoughts.)

Honest	Kind	Respectful
Confident	Gracious	Disciplined
Polite	Generous	Selfless
Joyful	Friendly	Grateful
Patient	Steady	Open-minded

TOOLS FOR GETTING UNSTUCK

....

Several types of life transitions leave us feeling severely stuck and uncertain. Even the best of us get stuck between a rock and hard place. When that happens, how do we get unstuck?

One of my favorite strategies for getting unstuck is answering this one question, "What's the next thing?" What I mean by this simple question is precisely…what would be the next, logical step I could take in the right direction? If I felt pressure to have it all figured out, that was too much. Often, we don't need to see the whole picture, but taking just one small step opens up a window of opportunity we wouldn't have otherwise seen.

Although it's hard to remember, many circumstances in life are beyond our control. It's a powerful choice, even when we feel we've been a victim to what has happened to us, to take a look at the scenario and decide how to take action and move forward. Moving forward might sound really different for many people. For some, it might be getting out of bed. For some, it might be asking hard questions and doing some internal work. For some, it might be taking action and hustling towards a big dream. Whatever that is for you, the past doesn't exist. It's time to decide to move forward.

What's my personal definition of "moving forward"?

What's my first step in the right direction?

What might be the next step after that?

Do I know the end goal?

Can I outline small steps to reach that overarching goal?

How does the next step affect my daily routine?

Will it require discipline or accountability?

❧ UNSTUCK IDEAS

STUCK	VS	UNSTUCK
Lost a job.		Apply for a new job. Research. Consider your options. Talk to people that can offer help in preparing a resume.
Just moved. Too much to do.		Hire extra help. Ask for help from friends or family. Or unpack the necessities and give yourself grace to transition at your own pace.
Ran out of money.		Consider ways you can earn more money. Sell items you own that are not necessity. Obtain assistance from organizations or government services available to you. Consider looking for a job that covers your cost of living. Set a budget and stick to it.
I need _____ .		Locate what you need. Identify who you can ask to help find what is needed.

❧ QUESTIONS TO HELP YOU GET UNSTUCK

What are the things you're most passionate about?

What kinds of resources do you need so you can move forward?

Where do you find those type of resources?

_____

_____

_____

_____

_____

_____

_____

If your life had no limits, what would you do?

_____

_____

_____

_____

_____

_____

_____

If your life had no limits, what would you choose to have?

Who do you admire the most? What can you learn from him/her?

Who do you know that would love to help you?

What do you like to do?

What do you not like?

How hard are you willing to work?

How does your faith impact your situation?

Where can you apply your faith to what you're facing right now?

THE FIVE BASIC NEEDS OF CHILDREN

....

Children process change much differently than adults or family units. While children are most resilient and adaptable, these five basic needs still must be met. During a season of change, it can be more challenging to have children in toe, yes. However, we can learn a thing or two from how children have the ability to see the world much differently than we do.

1. Safety
2. Nurture
3. Basic Trust
4. Belonging and Invitation
5. Someone to Love*

*From The Mom Factor By Dr. Henry Cloud and Dr. John Townsend

The good news? These needs are not tethered to a specific type of location. These needs can be met in a variety of home-like scenarios.

❧ CHILDHOOD NEEDS UNMET

In many families, the parents struggled and were unable to provide what the children needed. If you experienced a childhood with needs that went unmet, I'm sorry for your difficulties.

Although it would be a process, it's important to grieve that loss and decide how you can make the home you once needed. Examples of families where children's needs are being actively met will be an important piece of your healing. It will present you a visual, not to compare, but rather to use as a starting point for understanding what a healthy family dynamic looks like.

Take the time you need to consider these questions.

Did I have a healthy childhood?

....

....

What are my good childhood memories?

....

....

....

....

What are my bad childhood memories?

....

....

....

....

....

How does that help or hinder my ability to navigate adulthood well?

How can I provide a healthy and stable childhood for my children even when life is uncertain at times?

What resources can help me process my grief and challenges?

....

....

....

....

....

....

....

....

....

....

How can I own my story, lay it to rest and remake home now?

....

....

....

....

....

....

....

....

....

....

Is home a difficult word for me to hear?

How does that impact me today?

A FINAL WORD TO THE NAVIGATORS

....

Friends,

You did it. You are doing it. I mean, look! You've read this book. You're pouring your heart into living this transition to the best of your ability. And gosh, I'm just really proud of you.

Most people resist change because it feels like we're jumping off a cliff into a dark hole. Typically, the unknown is frightening. When I started this book, I said to you, "Let's jump!" And this entire book is my best effort to shed some light where it may feel dark. I jumped first so you can see...I made it.

Yes, I survived the worst-move-ever. Yes, I survived the sleepless nights and the job transition. I survived the long days, the loss of my hard-earned routines, and the uncertain freak-outs in the middle of the night. So far, I actually survived. Surprisingly, most days I forget the worst of it. If I can survive 100% of my worst days, you can, too. You really can. No matter what you are facing, I believe you will come out stronger and better than ever.

Looking back, all that really matters in the end is how far we've come. The rest is just a fleeting memory. And who we're becoming is just ahead, within reach.

I don't know your struggles. I don't know your ups and downs or your stories of failed plans. Our stories will be wildly different. But, even so, I want to thank you for using this little book to help you along the way.

You can do this. You are doing this. You are a gift to your family, your friends, your community, and more. And now you, too, are navigating your mess with grace and heart *and hope and patience and love and support... you're not alone.*

Home, after all, isn't a place. It's a heartbeat. As long as your heart is beating, you can make home, and be home, wherever you go. *I believe it with my whole heart.*

Carry on,

xo.

Brooke

less can be more. Homeless, but not hopeless. You got this.

Made in the USA
Columbia, SC
02 October 2018